CORBYNISM
WHAT WENT WRONG?

BY MARTIN THOMAS

Corbynism: What Went Wrong?
By Martin Thomas

Published by Workers' Liberty. June 2021

workersliberty.org

awl@workersliberty.org

020 7394 8923

20E Tower Workshops
Riley Road
London SE1 3DG

fb.com/workersliberty

twitter.com/workersliberty

instagram.com/workers_liberty

youtube.com/c/WorkersLibertyUK

Printed by Imprint Digital
Exeter
EX5 5HY

ISBN: 978-1-909639-54-6

Cover images: bit.ly/corb-cover (cropped) bit.ly/corb-back (cropped)

Contents

Introduction

On 12 September 2015 an excited crowd moved to Parliament Square to hear Jeremy Corbyn make his first street appearance as Labour leader by speaking at a demonstration for asylum-seeker rights. At the Queen Elizabeth Conference Centre, Corbyn had just been announced leader of the Labour Party by an election landslide. Young people there agreed that they must now get involved in week-by-week organising. Voting Corbyn for leader and waiting for him to become prime minister was not enough.

The shock of the 2008 economic crash, and the tension of the seven years of neoliberal recovery-via-austerity since, had finally stirred up a big left-wing response in Britain. The biggest new political surges since 2008 internationally had been right-wing (the pre-Trump but proto-Trump "Tea Party" in the USA from 2009; Modi's election in India, 2014…). Now in Britain there was something like the indignados movement in Spain (from 2011), Syriza in Greece (which had surged from 2011, won an election in January 2015, but then signed a new austerity deal in July 2015), or the Sanders movement in the USA (Sanders started his campaign for the 2016 Democratic nomination in April 2015). This was more sudden, but looked stronger than the others.

The left had, or had apparently, won the Labour Party, a party with some organisation in every corner of England, Wales, and Scotland, and with over a century of roots in and links into the British working class. Life had been dwindling or slight in the Labour Party for 20 years, since Tony Blair signalled a shift by abolishing its old socialistic Clause Four in 1995. In fact, dwindling grievously for 30 years, since Neil Kinnock consolidated his hold in the aftermath of the miners' defeat in 1985. Now Labour had come back to life. Its membership rose to nearly 400,000 by the end of 2015. It would remain above 400,000 through to 2021, and peak at nearly 600,000 in late 2017. Despite many moves by Blair and Brown to weaken Labour's ties to the trade unions, those ties had survived in some shape, and support from the big trade unions had been a factor in Corbyn's victory. The Tory party had won the general election in May 2015 on a manifesto of continued social cuts and with a vote increased above when they became the biggest party in the May 2010 election. Now the Tories looked not so strong at all.

A little over four years later, on 13 December 2019, Jeremy Corbyn announced he would resign as Labour leader. He eventually handed over to Keir Starmer on 4 April 2020. In the intervening months, which included the outbreak in Britain of the Covid-19 pandemic, he acted only as a caretaker, saying little. It was not a passing-on-the-baton full of honours. It was a rout. When a poll in December 2019 asked people how Corbyn was doing as leader of the Labour Party, 81% said "badly" or "very badly", and only 4% "very well". The nearest to a "Corbynite" candidate in the ensuing Labour leadership election, Rebecca Long-Bailey, did poorly, with a politically-limp campaign and 27.6% of the vote. The winner, Keir Starmer, did not stand as anti-Corbyn, praised Corbyn for making Labour an "anti-austerity party", and presented himself as left-wing. Yet his victory has been followed by a blanding-down of Labour criticism of the Tories; a turn to the right on many issues; a new flood of arbitrary suspensions of activists; and a decline in Labour Party life. Local meetings (even online) were banned on virus-precaution pretexts from March to July 2020, and in some though not all areas have shown only reduced life since then.

Labour Party membership in August 2020, on the most accurate count available, individual-member ballots distributed for the National Executive elections, was 495,961, not very different from June 2018, and probably higher than real figures before the June 2017 general election. Some left-wingers have quit, but most have stayed. The September 2019 Labour Party conference was the most left-wing since the 1980s. The human basis of that leftism is dismayed and demobilised, for now. Not disappeared. Or not yet.

The Black Lives Matter demonstrations in June and July 2020 showed that there are still lots of young people ready to come out on the streets for left-wing ideas; or, more accurately, those demonstrations, and the school student climate strikes peaking in September 2019, showed new generations of young leftists. An 18 year old marching to Kill The [Police] Bill in 2021 would have been only 12 when Corbyn won his 2015 poll. The pandemic and lockdown, from March 2020, stifled big industrial disputes, including a planned postal workers' strike which would have been Britain's weightiest industrial action for many years. But a spate of refusals to enter unsafe work areas — essentially, assertions of workers' control — running through 2020 strengthened union organisation and membership in many workplaces. Accumulated anger over the Tory government's floundering and bluster in the pandemic will fuel further revolt. We can't predict when and how. There is no return to dead calm. But the left that was jubilant and confident in September 2015 is dismayed and disarrayed now. A little over a year after Corbyn withdrew as leader, Labour did badly in the elections of 6 May 2021. The old operator Peter Mandelson seized on the occasion to demand a new push on the old Blairite programme of sidelining or neutralising Labour Party conference and marginalising the unions. There is potential to push back Mandelson and those in Starmer's inner circle who think like him, but the left is on the back foot. Something went wrong. This booklet explores why and how.

The real lost promise

The argument, in short, is this. The great promise opened by September 2015 was not, as too many thought, a smooth route to "JC4PM" (Corbyn as prime minister) and then to socialism. No such smooth route was ever possible. The great opening was for a rebuilding of the labour movement at the base, both ideologically and in organisation in workplaces and neighbourhoods. That rebuilding would have made many other things possible, including the election of a reform Labour government led by Corbyn and the implementation and consolidation of reforms. Without that rebuilding, the "JC4PM" strategy was never going to bring good fruit.

There was some rebuilding. For the first time in a long while, the Corbyn period showed that a left-led Labour Party, not obsessed with tracking the "centre ground", could be popular. It freed discussion to go beyond puzzling over what would go down well with "focus groups", and on to what was right and necessary. There was some conversion of 2015 voters for Corbyn who had previously been inactive into activists; some reaching out to bring in new activists; some reopening of discussion processes pretty much stifled since the 1990s; some ideological reorientation. Only, not nearly enough. Nowhere near enough to reach the "critical mass" required to produce a powerful-enough escalating interaction of workplace struggles; street action; day-to-day public campaigning; and week-by-week discussion, debate, education, and organisational rebuilding.

Corbynism ran aground, eventually, on two political issues which had been blind spots in the common-stock leftism of 2015: Brexit and antisemitism. Those and other blind spots could have been remedied by debate and education. Surely not without ructions and crises: but remedied, especially if more young people had been drawn into regular activity. They weren't. As we shall see later, Labour's youth and student wings if anything declined in the Corbyn period. "Adult" Labour Party organisations became more lively, but mostly with an influx of older people already "formed" politically by previous decades. Only a meagre culture of debate and education developed.

To see why, let's pick up the story from 2015, and first see how Corbynism kept afloat from then to 2019. We will then see how it became more and more fatally waterlogged.

How Corbyn won in 2015

Labour had done badly in the May 2015 general election. The Labour left had done especially badly. Before the May general election John McDonnell had attempted to assemble a "Left Platform" group to present a left profile there. The attempt flopped dismally. Activists around *Solidarity* and Workers' Liberty initiated a "Socialist Campaign for a Labour Victory". That got a reasonable response, but very much a minority one. Ed Miliband resigned as Labour leader.

The main candidates to replace him, Andy Burnham and Yvette Cooper, started to compete in promoting themselves as even more right-wing than they were already known to be. John McDonnell wrote that it was "the darkest hour that socialists in Britain have faced" for many decades.

"Darkest", as it turned out, was not accurate. It is easy to underestimate the potential of dispersed and thin-spread shifts to the left. Years of small meetings, difficult literature sales, and such can make left-wingers think that everyone out there is uninterested, when maybe we just haven't deployed enough energy to make left activity accessible and give it pulling power, and those "out there" haven't been confident enough to turn a tentative interest into consistent activity. Student protests in November and December 2010 had drawn over 50,000. Big marches had accompanied the public sector strikes over pensions in 2011, and maybe 400,000 joined the TUC demonstration in March 2011. The public-sector strikes were allowed by the union leaders to fade away into defeat; local anti-cuts campaigns big in 2010-11 dwindled in the years after; and the university campuses subsided from 2011; but demonstrations on cuts and on the NHS continued large. There had also been a slow-burning and unspectacular shift to the left within the Labour Party since 2010, with many activists quietly angered by Ed Miliband's retreat from the soft leftish promises on which he had won the leadership.

Burnham and Cooper miscalculated all that. Their pitch was that Labour had lost in May 2015 because it had been too left-wing, and they would pull Labour back to the right. A flurry among Labour members, mostly in cyberspace, demanded a left candidate for leader. No-one at that stage imagined a left candidate could win. Many thought there should at least be a voice of protest in the leadership battle. John McDonnell refused, and was cool on the whole idea of a left candidate. Ian Lavery refused; he had already opted for Andy Burnham. Jon Trickett refused. The left-wing journalist Owen Jones argued that the left should not try to run a candidate, because that would expose it to being "crushed". The pressure from Labour members was sufficient that, eventually, in a meeting of left MPs, McDonnell told Corbyn: "It's your turn", and Corbyn assented. Enough soft-left MPs, under pressure from their local members, agreed to nominate Corbyn that he reached the necessary MP-nominations quota with a few mavericks and a few right-wingers who thought that having Corbyn in the contest and defeated in plain view would boost the credibility of their favoured contestant.

"When Corbyn offered to stand", writes Alex Nunns in his book *The Candidate*, "he was volunteering — in all probability — for no more than a couple of weeks of lobbying and media appearances, a chance to raise the issue of austerity and, when he failed to make the ballot, to demonstrate that the leadership election rules were rigged against the left". Labour's right wing had in 2014 changed the rules for Labour leader elections to make them simple one-person-one-vote operations among Labour's members and "registered supporters". The right-wingers did that because, as they peered out at the populace through the opaque windows of the world of Parliament, lobbyists, the media, think-tanks, and PR, the only world many of them had known in adult life, it looked to them as if Blair-Brown-type babble commanded wide support which would help them outflank labour-movement activists. They were utterly wrong.

The right-wing pitch of Burnham's and Cooper's campaigns signalled to the union leaders a danger that they would be excluded from political influence even more thoroughly than under Blair. The union leaders had accommodated to Blair and Brown, though more vexedly from 2005 at least. But neither Burnham and Cooper was Blair. Neither commanded the deference a prime minister, or someone who looked like they would become prime minister soon, could get. Burnham and Cooper themselves may have thought that conciliating the union leaders was unnecessary, or even undesirable, bringing a danger of being stigmatised as "the unions' candidate". Unite leader Len McCluskey had initially favoured Burnham, but soon both the biggest unions, Unite and Unison, and many smaller unions, backed Corbyn. They did not get out many "affiliated supporter" votes for the ballot, but they provided money and resources and credibility for the Corbyn campaign.

15,800 people, many of them new to regular politics, volunteered for the Corbyn campaign. Starting from zero, it became a bigger operation than any of the establishment candidate campaigns. The Corbyn campaign, unexpectedly both for its organisers and for its opponents, became a condensation-point for a large cloud of political sentiment. Labour Party individual membership had fallen to an all-time low of 156,000 in late 2009. It ticked up to 194,000 by late 2010, with influxes, generally of people a bit to the left of the norm of the 2009 rump membership, after the 2010 election and after the election of Ed Miliband as a new leader seen as more union-friendly. The Blair-continuity candidate, David Miliband, had won a 44%-30% majority over his more soft-left brother among individual Labour members, and Ed Miliband won overall thanks to a 41%-28% lead among affiliated union members. But Labour membership then stagnated until 2015, at around 200,000. New people, almost all leftish, applied to join and rejoin as the 2015 leadership contest proceeded. Acting Labour leader Harriet Harman sent all Labour MPs the names of the recruits in their constituencies, and asked them to weed out known leftists. The Compliance Unit at Labour HQ barred hundreds or maybe thousands of recruits, and summarily expelled (without charge or hearing) maybe dozens of established members known to be left-wing; but eventually was overwhelmed by the scale of the influx.

294,000 individual members, almost a 50% increase on the figure before the

2015 general election, were entitled to vote for leader, and 246,000 of them voted. Even the pre-2010 members had edged leftwards. Corbyn won almost 50% of the individual-member votes, way ahead of Burnham on 23% and Cooper on 22%, as well as 58% of the affiliated union-member vote and 84% of the "registered supporter" vote. He might have won even if the electoral system had kept MPs' votes with one-third of the weighting.

By summer 2016, with a new leadership election, Labour membership was around 550,000, and it has remained around that level, with ups and down, ever since. There has been a drop since the early 2020 leadership election, but, so far anyway, no bigger than other fluctuations seen over the period 2016-20.

How Corbyn held on in 2015-16

Corbyn and his close associates faced difficult odds after the September 2015 leadership victory. The Tories had just had their first outright general election win for 23 years. Both the Parliamentary Labour Party and the Labour Party machine had over decades become stacked with right-wingers. The Labour Party's structure had been changed since the mid-1990s to make it difficult for the membership to prevail against the MPs and the machine. Corbyn's victory was the product of an unintended crack in that system.

In some ways, Corbyn's team did well against the odds. Labour MPs attempted a coup against him in June 2016, seizing as pretext on a lacklustre effort by Corbyn in the Brexit referendum of that month and a mediocre performance by Labour in the May 2016 local elections. (Labour's vote then was 2% up on 2015, and similar to 2014, but 7% down on 2012, which was a relevant comparator given the four-year cycles of local polling). 21 members of the Shadow Cabinet resigned (this was a Shadow Cabinet of those who had agreed to serve with Corbyn in September 2015, when many right-wingers had refused). 172 Labour MPs voted no confidence in Corbyn (with 40 voting against, and 17 abstaining or spoiling their ballots).

To his credit, Corbyn stuck it out and refused to resign. Most of the Labour-affiliated unions, including Unite, Unison, and CWU (but not GMB), stuck with him. Their leaders must have calculated that with Corbyn ousted, they would be back to the old days of Blair and Brown (or, after Falkirk, Ed Miliband), marginalised and disavowed. Thanks to union support, the National Executive decreed that Corbyn was automatically on the leadership ballot paper, without the impossible task of getting "enough" MPs to nominate him. The Labour right, confident enough to attempt the coup, proved not confident enough to complete it. Observing Burnham's and Cooper's rout in 2015, none of the big figures of the Labour right was confident to run. Instead they put forward Owen Smith, a figure obscure enough (they hoped) not to be tainted by the old regime. In the meantime, greater numbers of left-minded people had joined Labour. Smith ran a wretched campaign; and Corbyn was re-elected on

24 September with 60% of the vote, up from the 58% he'd had in 2015.

The September 2015 Labour Party conference had been eerily quiet. The delegates had been elected, the motions had been submitted, and the observers had booked their places, all before the Corbyn earthquake. The 2016 Labour Party conference, immediately following the second leadership election result, was a setback. Apparently distracted by the leadership election, the Corbyn team failed to take up a set of limited but useful democratic reforms to Labour Party structure which the affiliated unions were willing to back. Instead, the right wing, in a last-minute coup, pushed through a number of anti-democratic changes, in particular one declaring it a crime under Labour Party rules for councillors to vote to defy Tory government budget constraints. The "Corbynite" left wing from the constituencies provided little push in the opposite direction at the 2016 conference. That was not because it was too weak in numbers (though an impressionistic assessment says that the leftward shift among constituency delegates which developed across the Corbyn period, and reached its height in 2019, was still weak in 2016). It was not even because the left was not organised; rather, because of the way it had been organised. Momentum had been set up in late 2015 as an attempt to regroup the Corbyn leadership-campaigns' grass-roots support. For reasons which we will examine later, it ran itself more or less solely as a defence-guard for Corbyn. It was willing, and indeed effective, in getting out the Corbyn vote in the 2016 leadership election, but, for fear of embarrassing Corbyn, had no wish to push policy debates at the conference, or to clash directly with the big unions which had gone along with the anti-democratic rule changes. Momentum organised little at the conference itself, focusing instead on a fringe festival.

Corbyn's team signalled at the conference that they would not push to turn Labour against Trident replacement or against NATO, and would "bury" that issue for the coming years. Some of the shadow-cabinet resigners, Keir Starmer for example, then decided to cooperate with Corbyn again and wait for better times. There was an uneasy pause.

The June 2017 general election

In June 2017 the Tories called an early general election, hoping to increase their majority and so ease their difficulties with finding a Brexit formula. Corbyn's office wrote a manifesto focused on increased social spending and abolition of student tuition fees, to be financed by taxing the rich. Labour right-wingers, with the wounds they had incurred by pro-austerity stances in 2015 still raw, acquiesced. The manifesto evaded, or was downright poor on, Brexit, immigration, trade-union rights, but both voters and activists paid little attention. The Tories' campaign was wooden, promising only "strong and stable government", which voters could read as nothing but a "strong and stable" continuation of the social cuts rolling on from 2010, which by now were causing increasing anger. The Tories actually increased their score slightly, as the UKIP vote collapsed from 12.6% in 2015 to 1.8%, but lost their parliamentary majority. Labour improved its score from 25% of the electorate at the start of the campaign to 40% on polling day.

Few Labour right-wingers were now up for much beyond sitting out the remaining Corbyn years and preparing to regain ground when times became more favourable. Tom Watson, a right-winger elected as Corbyn's deputy in 2015 (on the basis of presenting himself as soft-left), tried to launch a right-wing Labour MPs' caucus, Future Britain, in March 2019, but nothing came of it. Watson withdrew from politics at the end of 2019. Ian McNicol, the right-wing General Secretary, resigned in March 2018 and was replaced by Corbyn supporter Jennie Formby. By December 2019, the Labour right wing was offering no resistance to a Labour manifesto markedly to the left of 2017's. In January-April 2020, all the candidates for Labour leader, and especially Keir Starmer, felt themselves obliged to pitch to the left. "Jeremy Corbyn made our party the party of anti-austerity and he was right to do so", declared Starmer. Far from collapsing in the face of right-wing Labour resistance, and despite its own weak starting point in September 2015, the Corbyn team pushed back the Labour right. The questions are: how did it manage it? And what were the weaknesses within the pushing-back which would lead to dismay, disarray, and retreat following so fast after December 2019?

The Leader's Office

One strength for the Corbyn team was inherited from previous decades, and especially from the Blair era. Since 1975 opposition parties have received official money processed through their parliamentary leaders. The personal office of the Leader of the Opposition has gradually become a weightier operation, with more full-time political operators, and more channels to the media, than the party's own HQ staff. Given a fair wind, the office appointed by Corbyn had a good chance of winning the battle of bureaucracies with the party HQ.

That strength came with weaknesses. As we'll see, when Corbyn won, he had no cohered "team" around him, no group of people who had developed cooperation and shared ideas in previous political action. The staff of his "Leader's Office" were mostly scraped together from the left margins of the politico-media-sphere and from networks at the top of bourgeois society. The key figure came to be Seamus Milne, who had been working for *The Economist* and *The Guardian* since 1981. Any involvement he had with rank-and-file labour movement activism dated back to his days as business manager of the ultra-Stalinist newspaper *Straight Left* in the late 1970s and early 80s (when this writer first met him: we were in the same economics evening class). Over time he drew Andrew Murray and Steve Howell, old associates from his Straight Left days, into the "Leader's Office". By 2019 the word was that in important meetings with other politicians, Corbyn would bring Milne with him, exchange pleasantries, and then let Milne do most of the important talking.

The Stalinist-heritage "Leader's Office" tilted Corbyn noxiously on issues like Brexit and antisemitism. And it was predisposed to have little interest in democratising the Labour Party. The Party structure did loosen up over the Corbyn years, so by 2019 annual conference was able to debate a lot more motions than before, and pass many in more radical forms than the platform wanted; but much of the structure and culture of the Blair years remained. Policy was still seen as being "developed" by backroom wonks, and then "announced" to a grateful world by shadow ministers, rather than primarily debated and decided by party structures. That remained true even for left-wing policies dropped into the December 2019 general election campaign at the last minute, free nationalised broadband and payments for women who had lost out on pensions through the Tories' accelerated increase in their state pension age. It hadn't crossed the minds of the "Leader's Office" to promote discussion of those measures in local Labour Parties, get motions brought to Labour conference, and decide them that way.

The "Leader's Office" depended for its clout on support from the big trade unions, especially from Unite, and indeed on exchange of personnel with them. Andrew Murray, chief of staff for Unite, became also a part-time worker in the "Leader's Office"; Karie Murphy, who became Executive Director of the "Leader's Office" in February 2016, was a close associate of the Unite leadership; Jennie Formby had been a Unite official before becoming Labour Party general secretary in March 2018.

The unions in the Corbyn period

Unions are the basic mass organisations of the working class. A strong say for them in the Labour Party is good. But this increased say for the trade unions was primarily increased lobbying-power for the top trade union officials. Trade-union say via elected union delegations at Labour Party conference controlling their leaders, or via elected and accountable union delegates in local Labour Party committees (a major factor in the 1980s) did not increase much in 2015-20. Trade unionists' participation in the Labour leadership election, which required under the new rules that they had opted in as "affiliated supporters", was meagre: 72,000 in 2015, 100,000 in 2016, 76,000 in 2020.

When the Unite union held a general secretary election in April 2017, left-wingers voted for the incumbent, Len McCluskey, because at that stage a victory for the right-wing candidate, Gerard Coyne, would probably have cut short the whole Corbyn experiment. The extent to which Unite's political activity lacked roots in the union's membership was shown by the result. McCluskey, who in his first contest, in 2010, had won with 101,000 votes to 53,000 for his runner-up, and in 2013 with 144,570 votes to 79,819, now got

Picturehouse workers fought for union recognition and better wages and conditions.

only 59,067 votes. He beat Coyne, who got 53,544, only narrowly. Only 130,071 voted, little more than half 2010's 240,000, in a union still claiming over a million members. There was no "Corbyn surge", no surge of left activism, in the unions to parallel the surge in the Labour Party.

Neither Corbyn nor any of the Labour left groups of 2015 could at will create such a surge within the unions. They could not change at will the fact that strike figures had been low since the public-sector pension strikes of 2011, and that they continued low in 2015-2020 — particularly low between April 2018 and October 2019. They could not change at will the fact that union membership, though still large (6.44 million in 2019), had been stagnant or falling for years. They could not even take particular credit from the fact that membership figures revived slightly in 2016-9: the steady if slow drop in unemployment figures from 2011 to 2019 was probably a bigger factor there.

The Corbyn leadership, and groups associated with it like Momentum, could have done a lot more to encourage working-class action, to get people to see union action as a way to win, to nurture new industrial activists, and to encourage people to chafe against and resolve to get rid of Britain's anti-union and anti-strike laws.

As we summed it up in early 2020 (*Solidarity* 534): "The party under Corbyn [had] done virtually nothing to support strikes and workers' struggles; and the same is true of most of its leadership. Shadow Chancellor John McDonnell is a partial exception. Corbyn himself has done much less than you might expect… He has been better than his [immediate] predecessors as leader — but that was a low bar to beat. He has not been a consistent presence, energetic campaigner or loud voice in support of strikes. He attended a protest for the last McDonald's strike — a politically safe and photogenic event, but not really an ongoing industrial dispute. In contrast, he largely steered clear of the much more sustained, disruptive and controversial rail strikes against Driver Only Operation… He attended a junior doctors' demonstration in 2017, but not any picket lines. Most perplexing of all is the Picturehouse dispute, going on for two years [2016-8] at multiple sites a few Tube stops from Parliament. Corbyn's office evaded repeated requests for him to join the picket lines... Corbyn did nothing to help the strike except a short written statement right at the end of the dispute".

Some left Constituency Labour Parties (CLPs) in the Corbyn years were active in support of strikes, like Sheffield Heeley CLP in support of railworkers' strikes against Driver Only Operation. Many left Labour members were active in strike support as individuals. Still, even at CLP level the rate of mobilisation was not high. There were more Labour Party banners on left demonstrations, against cuts, for the NHS, against Boris Johnson's attempt to "prorogue" Parliament in August-September 2019, on climate change in September 2019, and so on, than in the Blair-Brown or Miliband years; but nowhere near as many as had been on the streets in the Labour Party's previous left surge, in the early 1980s.

Corbynism on the streets. Or not?

The biggest left demonstrations of the Corbyn years, the big anti-Brexit demonstrations of October 2018 and March and October 2019, had some Labour politicians speaking, including John McDonnell in October 2019, some CLP banners, and, surely, many tens of thousands of left Labour Party members, but no official support or participation by the Labour Party.

When Michael Foot, a very faded sort of leftist by then, became Labour leader in 1980, he quickly had the Labour Party organise large protests against unemployment: 150,000 in Liverpool in November 1980, 50,000 in Glasgow in February 1981. He spoke at, and Labour Parties mobilised heavily for, the CND unilateral nuclear disarmament demonstration of October 1981, 250,000 strong, generally reckoned as the biggest demonstration ever in Britain to that date. In September 1982 Foot led a demonstration supporting a health workers' pay dispute. Corbyn's Labour Party had a weaker record on street protest than Foot's. Or even than Gaitskell's right-wing Labour Party of the mid-1950s. In November 1956 Gaitskell's Labour Party organised the biggest demonstration in Britain for 30 years, since the General Strike of 1926, to protest against the Tory government's invasion of Egypt to re-take the Suez Canal, which had been nationalised by the Egyptian government. The next year the London Labour Party called demonstrations on housing. Though Corbyn spoke at some protests, the Corbyn Labour Party organised no demonstrations in its own right.

The period leading up to Corbyn's election had been one of low strike levels, but also one of big street protests. Maybe 250,000 joined the People's Assembly anti-cuts protest in June 2015. Paradoxically, and surely not because of any constraints outside Labour's control, the increased political mobilisation into the Labour Party in the Corbyn years went together with a decline in street protests over cuts, the NHS, and so on.

Outside the leftish general election campaigns of 2017 and 2019, Corbyn's Labour did very little left-wing public campaigning. There was always some level of anti-cuts message; but not very vigorous. There was no coordinated campaigning against the major area of social cuts in those years, in local government. There was not even the sort of campaigning which appeared briefly in the early Miliband years, in which some Labour councils made cuts but at the same time publicly appealed for pressure to make the Tory government restore funding. "Left-wing" Labour councils were those who made fewer cuts, perhaps, had "progressive procurement", used adroit financial maneouvres to build or buy a bit of council housing. There were local campaigns against cuts in particular councils (libraries, children's centres, etc.) in the Corbyn years, with local Labour Party members taking part, but usually with support from only a harassed minority of Labour councillors. From the top of the Labour Party, the anti-cuts message often narrowed down into a focus on opposition to *police* cuts. That was particularly noticeable in the high-profile and narrow-margin by-election in Peterborough in June 2019, conducted with a "Corbynite" candidate and with the "Leader's Office" by then having good control of the party apparatus. In all those ways, the Corbyn leadership, and much of the "official" Corbyn left in the Labour Party, failed to encourage working-class action, to get people to see union and street action as a way to win concessions even while the Tories still ruled, and to nurture and draw in new industrial and community activists. The worst of that was Corbyn Labour's more or less complete failure to draw in and organise activists from the large pool of youth support for Corbyn shown in 2015, 2017, and 2019.

Labour and young people in the Corbyn period

Anecdotally, Corbyn's most enthusiastic support in 2015 was among young people. In the 2017 election around 62% of 18-24 year olds voted Labour. Only 27% voted Conservative. (Figures from Ipsos MORI polling data.) 25% of over-65s voted Labour, while 61% voted Conservative. In the 2019 election the difference was even greater, with a 43-point Labour lead among the youngest voters, and a 47-point Tory lead among the over-65s. Young people have long been more likely to vote Labour than older people in British general elections: the pattern goes back to at least 1974, probably further. There has never before been so marked an age gradient. Few of the leftish young people joined Labour. By 2018 a survey by academics at Queen Mary University showed that only 4% of Labour's members were aged 18-24, a smaller percentage (though a bigger absolute number) than the Tories' 5%. Even the 25-34 age group, where a sizeable minority must have been formed politically by the 2010-11 student revolt over fees and Education Maintenance Allowance, had only 12% of Labour members, better than the Tories' 9% but worse than the Lib Dems' 14%. The 35-44 age group, where we might hope for numbers formed by the "alternative globalisation" movement around 2000, was no better represented, with 12% of Labour members compared to the Lib Dems' 17%.

More Labour Party members were over 65 than were under 44. Labour members' average age was 53, and 56% of them were over 55. The "median" Labour member was pushing 60, probably someone who had been "formed" politically in late-teenage and early-20s years around the late 1970s and early 80s. Labour Party and left activity shrivelled a lot from the 1990s up to 2015, so statistically that "median" member had probably been largely out of political activity for decades, beyond occasional demonstrations against the invasion of Iraq in 2003, or against austerity after 2010. Anecdotally, many "returners" would be retired or near-retirement, after job promotions which had made them more prosperous than they had been in say 1980, and with their children if any now grown-up and no longer economically dependent.

The Corbyn era was, as we shall see, part of a distinctly new epoch of "social media" politics; it was also part of an epoch distinctly new in another way, the first time in human history that over-60s had been more prosperous on average than people in their 20s, and many of them still in good health. A 65-year-old may be more dynamic than a 25-year-old. But the 65-year-olds or 55-year-olds of the Corbyn levy had been politically trained, mostly, by being out of political activity (apart from the occasional demonstration or such) since they were first formed politically as leftists in the 1970s or 1980s. It was a different sort of influx from the one the Labour Party had after 1979, dominated by young or early-middle-age people formed politically by, and coming straight from, activity in strikes, anti-cuts campaigns, anti-racist protests, tenants' movements, and university campus agitation. Political inactivity "trains" us politically just as much as political activity trains us, only in a different way: towards impatience with argument, a desire for quick answers "from above", a propensity to be easily deterred by obstacles. It is possible to reverse that training. Some Corbyn-era "returners" did that. But it is difficult, especially in the absence of a lively-enough influx of radical youth to re-educate the older ones.

In 2016, the 18-24 age group among Labour Party members was the only one to return a majority for Owen Smith against Corbyn. Labour Students remained under the control of the Blairite Labour right throughout, until it was officially derecognised in September 2019. The student Labour rightists used extravagant bureaucratic manipulation to keep their control; but they got away with it. There was no strong coordination of left-wing campus Labour

Clubs to counter them. Most campus Labour Clubs remained weak and dull. The Momentum "youth" operation paid little attention to campus Labour Clubs, or even to building Young Labour groups in constituencies, instead focusing on winning the machinery of Young Labour. Young Labour was indeed "taken over" by the left. That was not a huge shift. A left-winger, Sam Tarry, had been elected chair of Young Labour as far back as 2009-11. Young Labour sided with the left in opposing the Collins Report in 2014. In the Corbyn years, a sort of left took over more thoroughly. One measure was London Young Labour. The left took over from the right at a conference in February 2018. The conference was marred by Stalinistic behaviour from the left, aimed especially against Workers' Liberty, but in broad terms the left won. There were nearly 400 at that conference, convened by the outgoing right-wing leadership. The first conference under the new left-wing leadership, in April 2019, had only 70 to 100 there, and managed to consider only one motion (a pro-Brexit motion, pushed through with almost no debate). Neither Young Labour nor Labour Students got anywhere near developing into the sort of open, easy-going, lively, friendly environment which young activists need to check out political ideas and activities. Where they developed some activity, it was almost always of twenty-somethings, inhospitable to teenagers.

The Corbyn leadership, Momentum, youth, and activism

On one level, what happened with Labour and young people in 2015-9 was a failure of the leadership. Corbyn, McDonnell, and their associates, even without having much prior "rank-and-file" organisation behind them, could at will have promoted a large growth of Young Labour groups and student Labour Clubs by touring the country and speaking. The Labour right could not have stopped them. Evidently they were too preoccupied with day-to-day firefighting with their opponents among the MPs and the Labour HQ officials to do that, and their "Leader's Office" had no interest.

What about the grassroots left? It started off weak, as the whole left was weak in 2015. The young Labour left was able to launch "Labour Young Socialists" (LYS) at a conference of 140 in September 2015, with Workers' Liberty a significant force in making it happen. Then LYS faded. Its space was taken over by Momentum Youth and Students, launched at a not-much-bigger conference (200) in June 2016, but with the imprimatur of Momentum. MYS at first had a committee fairly evenly balanced between the Stalinistic trends whose record in London Young Labour was described above, and more LYS-type people. Over the next year and a half, the Stalinistic trends manipulated the committee (for example, by adding new regional reps) to gain and hold control, and ran down MYS activity, until finally MYS's social media (its chief self-expression) were cut off by the Momentum office in January 2018 as so grossly Stalinistic as to be embarrassing. It is difficult to avoid the conclusion that more energy and vigour from us, from the radical anti-Stalinist left, or just us being a bit more numerous to start with, could have made at least some difference back then. How much, we can't know. The outcome was that a Stalinistic left, with lots of its leaders already embedded in the "wonkosphere" of parliamentary assistants, think-tanks, NGOs, union political departments, etc., became a dead weight against the possibility of recruiting youth into Labour in any numbers.

Overall, despite the Corbyn-era Labour Party's endless self-congratulation about how membership had grown, its new mobilisation of activists was weaker and lower-temperature than the aggregate figures suggested. There was much self-congratulation about numbers coming out to campaign for Labour in the 2017 and 2019 general elections. They were surely better than the pitiful turnouts in the Blair-Brown government years, but the scale even of Labour Party electoral activity, let alone of Labour Party campaigning on social and political issues, was in many areas weak compared to the 1980s or even, probably, to 1996-7. In 2018 the Queen Mary University study cited above found that, of those who were Labour Party members on paper, 41% had had no face-to-face (rather than electronic) contact with other Labour Party members, although the survey was done straight after the 2017 general election, which must have mobilised some previously inactive people. Only 28% said they had "frequent" face-to-face communication. Asked how they'd come to join, only 4% said they had joined because approached by someone from their local Labour Party — a much smaller percentage than for the Tories (15%) or Lib-Dems (10%). 93% had approached the Labour Party (i.e., presumably, electronically) on their own initiative.

The demographic limitations of the Corbyn surge would weigh heavy. The first question in 2015, however, was about how the influx would shake out and be grouped politically. The demographic limitations shaped political limitations; political limitations shaped the demographic limitations.

Corbyn and socialism

"Lewisham for Corbyn", "Sheffield for Corbyn", and similar groups had sprouted in 2015, a beginning of a regroupment of the left. The central running of the Corbyn campaign, from mid-June to mid-September, was ad hoc, understandably without formed democratic structures, but without bureaucratic hostility to the local groups, often initiated by activists well to the left of the Corbyn inner circle.

Jeremy Corbyn himself was well respected among left-minded activists and semi-activists, but for decades had (unlike the other best-known left Labour MP, John McDonnell) been much more an individual parliamentary dissident (and a supporter of popular campaigns in his constituency) than an organiser and ideologist with and among the left groups. I summarised his trajectory in an article in *Solidarity* 370, 3 July 2015. Corbyn had become a visible figure in the

Labour left as it revived in 1979, writing for *Socialist Organiser*, a forerunner of *Solidarity*. Then "he was a young union official and a left-wing Labour councillor in Haringey, north London". *Socialist Organiser* was a campaigning paper, with a wide range of contributors. But "its broad coalition subscribed to much clearer and more radical ideas than the general 'broad left' of the labour movement, which in those days was dominated by the Communist Party and its influence. It called for 'working-class action to raze the capitalist system down to its foundations, and to put a working-class socialist system in its place... to make the decisive sectors of industry social property, under workers' control'.

"The coalition around *Socialist Organiser* broke up in 1980 over choices for left-Labour councils (then numerous) facing Thatcher's Tory government. We [the forerunners of *Solidarity*] argued for them to use the town halls as platforms to mobilise for confrontation. Others argued for them to 'gain time' by increasing rates (local property taxes) to offset cuts in central government finance. The core rate-raisers [eventually, in late 1980] went off to produce [an alternative publication] *Labour Briefing* (two rival journals of that name continue today)... The main document in which [they] laid out their basis for splitting from *Socialist Organiser* was signed by [those who would become the core *Briefing* people] and one other person, Jeremy Corbyn". Yet Corbyn was less factional about the split than others. He wrote often for *Socialist Organiser* for many years after, and then drifted away gradually, rather than "breaking" with us.

"In 1983 Corbyn became Labour MP for Islington North. He has been a consistent rebel in Parliament against the Labour leadership. His local record of support for workers' and community struggles, including against local Labour council adminstrations, is excellent. But Jeremy Corbyn's broader politics have changed. Today he writes regularly for the *Morning Star*, the paper linked to the Communist Party of Britain, which bills him as 'a friend of the Star'. People voting for Corbyn for Labour leader will be voting to support battles against cuts, to solidarise with immigrants, and to uphold the right to strike. That's good. But to build something solid out of it, we also need broader political ideas. And, there, the ideas and the spirit of the *Morning Star* will undermine us as much as in 1979...

"Jeremy Corbyn is surely a socialist. But in his articles for the *Morning Star* he rarely or never says that. He calls for a 'popular movement against cuts'. He advocates 'raising taxes for the very richest, collecting tax from corporations'. But not social ownership of industry. Not expropriating the banks. Not workers' control... Corbyn rarely uses the word 'socialist', but he has commented on Chavez's Venezuela, Evo Morales's Bolivia, and Castro's Cuba as if they are, more or less, models of a future society. That model of a future society is one to which workers in a country like Britain could never be won. Or, if they were won to it, it would be a grievous sidetrack, similar to the winning of millions of French and Italian workers after World War Two to the USSR as a model of future society".

Corbyn's reluctance to speak about socialism was probably connected with declining conviction that socialism, in any comprehensive sense, as distinct from signifying a "social" outlook and resistance to excesses of capitalism, was even viable or credible.

In 1935 Hugh Dalton, soon to become chair of the Labour Party and then Chancellor in the 1945 Labour government, wrote a book, *Practical Socialism in Britain*, to explain the official Labour Party programme produced as the party reoriented after Ramsay MacDonald's betrayal and Labour's defeat in the 1931 general election (a more crushing affair than in 2015: down to 52 seats, from 287 in 1929). The goal was the elimination of "private profit-making". "It is the chief historic aim of Socialism to transfer to public ownership private property rights in the means of production". There should also be "workers' control". "Only in a Socialist society can labour cease to be a mere commodity, bought and sold in the market, hired and fired at the will of the boss... only in such a society can the worker be fully endowed with human dignity and civic status".

Dalton remonstrated against what he called "doctrinaires" that "Socialism is a quantitative thing. It is a question, not of all or nothing, but of less or more... We may measure the degree in which any particular community is Socialist by the relative extent of the 'socialised sector', and of the 'private sector', in its economic life". He presented the existing state structure, top civil service, police, monarchy, and all, as a neutral instrument which could be used bit by bit to expand the "socialised sector". Bit by bit was better because more "practical"; and, anyway, Dalton insisted, the British people had a "distrust of logic... distaste for doctrine... cult of the practical... gift for compromise". Neither fascism nor communism, he blandly insisted, could rise in Britain. "Neither a Saklatvala nor a Mosley seems to find his spiritual home in British public life".

So workers should be patient and wait for Dalton and his colleagues to do things bit by bit! There was a definite aim for the "bit by bit". Room was thus opened for others to argue that the state machine was not neutral, that the tiger of capitalism could not be skinned claw by claw, and that logic and theory were as necessary in Britain as elsewhere.

From 1923 to 1987 (even in the right-wing 1950s) Labour's manifestos always contained some vague promise of socialism as a vision, long-term aim, or guiding value. "Further achievements towards a really Socialist Commonwealth" (1924); "Socialism provides the only solution for the evils" (1931); "ultimate purpose... the establishment of the Socialist Commonwealth" (1945); "policy based on the ethical principles of Socialism" (1959); "programme of socialist reconstruction" (1983)... When "pragmatists" and "revisionists" like

Anthony Crosland, in the mid-1950s, sought to remove Labour's notional commitment to bring all the "commanding heights" of productive wealth into public hands, they did so with the argument that welfare spending and trade-union gains could bring society to a socialist condition of relative equality and the remaining privately-owned sector in the "mixed economy" would be so hemmed in as not to disrupt that.

In the 2017 manifesto, the words "socialist" or "socialism" were not used at all; in the 2019 manifesto, "socialism" appeared once, and not to state an aim, rather to describe what already exists in the NHS. There was no attempt to say the same thing in different words, either. As general summaries, we got only "For the Many, Not the Few" (a phrase coined by Tony Blair), and "Real Change" (but who advocates illusory change?). The "official" Corbynite Labour left, Momentum, too rarely spoke of socialism. At most it would (and still does) call for "transformative" change. But what is that other than a way of saying "transformative transformation"? Or just "transformation"? Or just "change"? Even Starmer's new right-wing general secretary, David Evans, is happy to recommend "transformational" change.

The 2019 manifesto included a good few radical demands. But they were dropped into the manifesto only a few weeks before polling day, and given a quick boost on social media, with no substantial prior campaigning for them over the previous years, and sometimes without even prior discussion of them at Labour conferences. No wonder many of those demands brought the reaction: "Sounds good. But do they really mean all this? Does it hold together?"

The well-known academic economist Geoff Hodgson wrote in 2016: "In 2015 [Corbyn] was reported in the *Mirror* newspaper as saying that socialism 'is an obvious way of living. You care for each other, you care for everybody, and everybody cares for everyone else. It's obvious, isn't it?'... I have little else to go on. Apart from some gestures in favour of nationalisation, and some sentimentality for the pre-Blair version of Labour's Clause Four, I can find no fuller account of what Corbyn's 'socialism' means".

The reader, especially if one of those who remember Hodgson as a socialist and a member of our own group at the end of the 1960s, will be put off by the smugness of his subsequent explanation that socialism is impractical because economic life is too complicated, and that recommending it can only produce "a fanaticism that can crush all traces of liberal tolerance".

Hodgson does show that Corbyn's version of socialism provided much less traction and leverage for debate and enlightenment than did Dalton's of 1935. Less, too, than Bernie Sanders' in the USA. Sanders calls for an economy which "works for" the working class and the middle class ("middle class" meaning, in the USA, better-off workers in stable jobs), not just for "big-money" interests. He calls for a "political revolution", and for mobilisation ("Not me.

Us"). He is trenchant on central particular demands like single-payer health care and laws to facilitate union organisation. His platform is inadequate in Marxist terms, and yet affords many hooks for further political development. Sanders' campaigning since 2015 has spurred many young people to move beyond Sanders' own limits and towards more defined socialist ideas. There is something there similar to what Marx wrote about the big movement that developed briefly around Henry George's campaign for public ownership of land in the 1880s. "That the first programme of this party is still confused and highly deficient, that it has set up the banner of Henry George, these are inevitable evils but also only transitory ones. The masses must have time and opportunity to develop and they can only have the opportunity when they have their own movement". "Theoretically the man... is utterly backward! ... [but his book] is significant because it is a first, if unsuccessful, attempt at emancipation from the orthodox political economy"... "and also actually on account of the vast extent of big landed property".

By 2015 many mainstream bourgeois figures wanted to soften neoliberalism. Now Boris Johnson blusters about "levelling up". Corbyn was, of course, more drastically and credibly "anti-austerity", but his stance did not breach a previously all-enveloping orthodoxy as dramatically as George's demands did in their own way. Corbyn Leader's Office, once in post, never had the focus or consistency of campaign on pivotal demands that Sanders has had. The message was general, and with a cloudiness which afforded few ideological stepping-stones.

Corbyn did a debate at the Oxford Union on socialism in 2013, and his speech can be heard on YouTube. He argues only for of universal health care, "protection from destitution", and every child being able to attend school without payment, plus the general moralising thought that socialism is about us "all caring for each other and supporting each other". He counterposes this socialism not to actual contemporary capitalism (with its actual, if inadequate, schools and NHS and welfare benefits) but to "Victorian free-market capitalism" with "no public provision of any service". When challenged by a Tory about Stalinist Eastern Europe, Corbyn fends him off only by disavowing any wish to defend "Stalin's strange views", and not by explaining that the Stalinist counter-revolution created a class society as remote from socialism as ordinary contemporary capitalism, indeed more so.

On the evidence, the Corbyn of 2015 had become heavily waterlogged, ideologically, by the decades in which the seas of Thatcherism and Blairism lapped around him. So had many of those who would become his associates around the "Leader's Office", and many of those in the constituencies who "returned" to left Labour politics after 2015.

That the "Corbyn surge" started around limited ideas — "against austerity", but not much more — was inevitable given the previous decades. Large and strong political movements grow not on day-to-day "immediate" issues, but mostly on big ideas, which can inspire and guide the sort of activism which persists, learns, and develops despite the inevitable "immediate" defeats. Corbyn's victory in 2015 opened new doors for discussing those big ideas. But pushing those doors fully ajar, and filling the space beyond them, would have to depend on impetus "from below", with little help from the "above" of the Corbyn leadership.

"False brothers"

The vagueness and lack of conviction in Corbynite socialism left it not only limited, but vulnerable to ideological colonisation by the "false socialisms" generated over the 20th century, notably those shaped at one remove or another by Stalinism. This factor would be critical in Corbyn Labour's fiascos over Brexit and over antisemitism.

"On some issues publicly (and possibly on many privately)", I continued in my 2015 assessment, "Corbyn is better than the *Morning Star*. He supports Tibet's national rights, he opposed Russia's seizure of Crimea and 'Russian militarism' in Ukraine. In the *Independent* (10 June 2015) he wrote: 'There are strong arguments for staying in the EU', while making reasonable criticisms of the EU as it exists. But on international politics, mostly, he limits himself to deploring military moves by the US and its allies and appealing for peace. So, for example, he expresses 'concern over human rights in Iran'. He notes the 'appalling human rights record of the Syrian regime'. He opposed Hamas's rocket attacks on Israel, and seems, though it is not clear, to support a two-states settlement in Israel-Palestine. The result is as with the more-or-less pro-Stalinist [but not fully Stalinist] left of the era between the 1960s and 1989-91. Repression in the Stalinist states? Reprehensible invasions? Bad. But they would shrug sadly at those things, rather than denouncing them loudly, because, they said, to denounce might help the 'cold warriors'. Never be 'anti-Soviet'! In truth socialists needed to oppose US and British imperialism, and simultaneously denounce Stalinism with vigour, and some did. The 'sad shrug' approach only compromised and discredited the leftists who took that line, and increased demoralisation after 1991. We should not copy the approach with Hamas in place of the USSR".

Corbyn's main engagement with the organised left in the run-up to the 2015 election had been with the Stop The War Coalition (STW). He was involved from 2002, then chair of STW from 2011 to 2015, stepping down when he was elected Labour leader. In STW he worked with Andrew Murray, a Communist Party member who became Chief of Staff for the Unite union in 2011 and would later join Corbyn's Leader's Office; with George Galloway; and with Socialist Workers Party people, the main ones among whom would quit the

SWP in 2010 to form a small group, Counterfire, with an orientation closer to the *Morning Star* than the SWP and backroom work for STW and the People's Assembly as its main activity. STW organised big demonstrations in 2002-3 against the US-led invasion of Iraq. Our chief criticism of its operation then is that it chose to promote the Muslim Association of Britain (a small group linked to the political-Islamist Muslim Brotherhood) as co-sponsor of the protests, together with the Campaign for Nuclear Disarmament (in whose inner circles the *Morning Star* was then influential). Between 2003 and 2015 STW became a smaller group, protesting not so much about "the" war as about US-aligned military operations, while silent about the wars of powers at odds with the USA.

Momentum

People who voted for Corbyn were clear that they were voting against the social cuts imposed by the Tories since 2010; against anti-migrant policies, at least the gross ones operated by the Tories since 2012 under the slogan "Hostile Environment"; against a repeat of the Iraq invasion (but the Tories had already pulled the last British troops out of Iraq in 2011); against the new restrictions on trade-union action in the Trade Union Bill introduced in July 2015, which would become the Trade Union Act 2016; against university tuition fees. Some of what they were voting for was clear, too. More social spending. A better-funded NHS, free of privatisation and marketisation. At least some renationalisation of utilities. Some more democracy in the Labour Party, where rank-and-file input, and to a large extent even union-leadership input, had been curtailed since Tony Blair became leader in the mid-1990s.

Corbyn's campaign had assembled the largest political mobilisation for decades on that axis, in, unavoidably, only a loose, ad hoc, and provisional way. A core question after September 2015 was whether that mobilisation could organise itself; discuss its positive programme and define it in a more rounded way; and work out at least the beginnings of a shared idea of ways and means to get there, beyond just hoping that a new leader would help. That depended, as political progress in the Labour Party had always depended, on organising the left at the rank-and-file level.

The inner circle of Corbyn's leadership campaign knew that, in their own way. Some of them now ceased direct public activity as they took jobs in the "Leader's Office" or elsewhere around the leadership, but one of them, Jon Lansman, set up a new movement, Momentum, only four weeks after Corbyn's victory.

Lansman described himself politically as a "Dererite", after Vladimir Derer, the founder in 1973 and long-time leader of the Campaign for Labour Party Democracy (CLPD). Derer had been a Trotskyist, and retained some ideals and ideas typical of Trotskyism, for example supporting the Polish workers and Solidarnosc in 1980-1, but coupled those with a sort of new Fabianism. We would get socialism by pushing Labour bit by bit to the left, through adroit alliances with the party middle ground and a stubborn focus on rule changes to improve party democracy. Lansman had come into high-profile politics in 1980 when, as a recently-graduated student, he had been nominated by CLPD to be the secretary of the united-left Labour Party democracy movement of that time, the Rank and File Mobilising Committee (RFMC), working alongside John Bloxam of *Socialist Organiser* (a forerunner of *Solidarity*), as RFMC organiser. Lansman was also a major figure in Tony Benn's 1981 deputy leadership campaign. Lansman had been out of all but local Labour politics for a long while before returning in 2010 and becoming central again in CLPD. We, Workers' Liberty, had worked closely with him in the 2014 campaign against the Collins Report (a move by the Miliband leadership to reduce trade-union leverage in the Labour Party). Lansman would separate from CLPD early in the Corbyn era, driven by differences over antisemitism and CLPD's resentments of Momentum.

The writer met Lansman for a conversation about his plans shortly before Momentum was publicly launched. To my surprise, what Lansman explained to me was a different model from any Labour left assemblage of the past. This, he said, would be a "social movement", not limited to Labour Party members. The *Guardian* (8 October 2015) had been briefed that "the group anticipates many thousands of people who are not Labour members or supporters will be involved in the wider social movement through their communities and workplaces". And the new movement, said Lansman, couldn't have even the ramshackle sort of democratic structure (conferences, elected committees) that those Labour left assemblages have usually had. It would be too big for that. As a sort of model, Lansman cited 38 Degrees. 38 Degrees was and is a left-wing movement which sees itself as exceptionally progressive, democratic, and attuned to "people power", declaring that its "campaigns are chosen and led by our three million members". But those "members" are just people who have signed up to its e-list. There are e-consultations about the choice of campaigns, but voting figures from those consultations are never (as far as I can find) published, and almost surely only a tiny fraction of the three million take part. There are no conferences or elected committees. In practice everything is decided by its 30-40 office staff, paid between £26,000 (for "interns") to above £50,000 (for "higher" staff: no figures seem to be available for the highest). There is also a "board" of worthies which meets, on its own description, only a few times a year. 38 Degrees was floated on money from charitable trusts and foundations in 2009, but now subsists on donations from the minority of its three million "members" who choose to make them. 38 Degrees mostly does e-petition campaigns, though it says that it "sometimes... acts offline, like visiting an MP or minister, taking out ads in newspapers, holding public

Jon Lansman's Momentum group abjured the democracy which Lansman himself had previously campaigned for. Image: bit.ly/Mom-Lans

meetings or fundraising for legal action". Fundamentally, members pay money so that the office can do politics (of an NGO-y sort) on their behalf.

We commented: "Momentum has so far been advertised as an autonomous movement open to all, Labour and non-Labour — a pantomime horse group combining the functions of Labour left caucus and '38 Degrees' type internet link-up. We doubt such a catch-all conception is viable…" And yet, despite the notional "open to all" policy, as of then "no-one (except presumably 'the Momentum team' [self-appointed, which was sending out electronic messages to the Corbyn-supporter database]) [could] join. And in some areas Momentum [was] taking the form of Facebook pages run by the self-elected". We called for a "clear Labour-focused remit", though with openness to working with non-Labour leftists in campaigns and on issues, and "a clear democratic structure".

Lansman also said to me, on more "Dererite" lines, that Momentum would aim to win the institutions of the Labour Party. He was cool but not hostile when I argued for a priority to recruiting new members to CLPs, Young Labour, and Labour Students, and organising them for local activity. My suspicion was and is that the "38 Degrees" model was handed down to him by Corbyn and McDonnell and others in their inner circle, rather than being his own. That circle thought (or seemed to think, judging from their public statements) that they could sidestep the problems which they had faced inside the Labour Party structures for two decades before 2015 by going round those structures and through the "social movements". Possibly the "projects" launched by Corbyn ("Peace and Justice Project") and by McDonnell ("Claim the Future") since April 2020 are new (though weak) attempts to reprise that perspective.

The other logic operating as Momentum was launched in October 2015 was that of ownership of the means of production, or rather ownership of the means of electronic communication. The Momentum office, or registered companies controlled by people in the Momentum office, owned the mass of contact data got from Corbyn's leader campaign. And for the sort of politics based largely on electronic communication rather than in-person meetings or action, those data are the "means of production" of politics. Through its whole history Momentum has operated primarily by the office mobilising people by electronic communication for internal Labour Party elections and to work for Labour in public elections, notably 2017 and 2019. It has been difficult for local Momentum groups to get local contact data from the office (data-protection laws being cited as the reason).

At its launch date, Momentum was nominally run by a "board" of MPs (we never found out, or at least I never found out, who), but in practice it has always been run by the office. In 2016 repeated lobbying and protest forced the calling of some regional and national meetings, and the creation of a national steering committee. The meetings adopted some good policies, notably against Brexit, against the continuing no-charge-or-hearing exclusions of leftists, against Trident replacement, and against antisemitism, but the office never published them. In that period we, Workers' Liberty people, were still able to meet and discuss with Lansman. I think we may even have shifted him somewhat on the issue of antisemitism. On democratic structures, he remained reluctant. If the office didn't keep control, it would be impossible to win the affiliation to Momentum of the Unite union, and to keep good working relations with the "Leader's Office". He mused: "Whatever you think about it, you have to work with the Communist Party. Vladimir [Derer] used to say that". Even then Lansman was openly discontented with the "Leader's Office". Later he would seek our backing in Momentum on the grounds that the more Stalinoid groups in Labour's top circles, linked most closely to Unite union HQ and the Skwawkbox blog, were intent on ousting him.

In September 2016 Momentum organised very little for Labour Party conference (the structures were not responsive enough for members' pressure to organise to produce results). It did put effort into a fringe festival organised semi-autonomously as The World Transformed. TWT was big, but Momentum-left speakers had been largely excluded from its platforms, and no left literature stalls were allowed inside. When we set up a Workers' Liberty stall in the street outside, the event organisers "instructed" us that we must pack up and move away. We refused point-blank, and eventually they let it go. But they had tried. Meanwhile the *Morning Star* was billed as a sponsor of the event, and was distributed as a free give-away inside it!

The Momentum coup of January 2017

It still looked as if Momentum was being pushed, slowly, reluctantly, towards a conference and a democratic structure. Then on the evening of 10 January 2017 Jon Lansman and the office organised a coup, abolishing all Momentum's committees and structures, and returning direct control to the office. Notionally, since February 2017, a part-elected "National Coordinating Group" has overseen the office. Since the Forward Momentum slate victory in the Momentum NCG elections of July 2020, there may be more supervision of the office by some NCG officers, but the NCG as such is still weak and opaque. No facility existed, or exists, for national discussion or debate in Momentum, other than a slight opening in periodic elections for the elected seats on the NCG. In the first NCG elections, 42% (of a 34% turnout, i.e. 14% of Momentum's membership, then given as 21,000) voted for a pro-coup slate for the elected positions; but the electoral system worked to give that slate almost a clean sweep.

The nearest to a public explanation of the coup was a message by Jon Lansman to CLPD: "sectarian elements on the Left wish to turn Momentum from a broad alliance it was intended to be, seeking to maintain the broad centre-left coalition that elected Jeremy Corbyn to support his administration, democratise the party along the lines long advocated by CLPD, and help Labour win elections into a hard-Left organisation reminiscent of the LRC designed to put pressure on Jeremy from the left..." Lansman was, he said, standing up for a silent majority of Momentum against "Trotskyist and other sectarian organisations". The dissolving of Momentum's structures would allow it to avoid a "battle for two months in the run up to a planned national delegate conference". We responded that a healthy Labour left must have discussion and democracy, not be tied to unquestioning support of the leadership. "Momentum would have contributed more, not less, if it had actively promoted a left Remain vote, free movement across borders, opposition to Trident renewal. It would be stronger now if its national office as well as its local groups had campaigned in support of workers' disputes like at Picturehouse, and for the NHS. It would have done better if (as we urged) it had organised a presence at Labour conference 2016. It would be healthier if it had had a proper discussion on left antisemitism (in which Jon Lansman and we would have been broadly on the same side), rather than trying to quell the issue administratively. All those things are not 'sectarian' caprices, but would have happened if Momentum had been allowed to develop 'normally', democratically... Some people have stopped attending Momentum meetings. But not because of political debate. Rather, because so many meetings have been dominated by bureaucratic obstruction and battles against it..."

On 11 March, 200 Momentum members, including 80 or 90 delegates from local Momentum groups, came to an anti-coup Grassroots Momentum conference. We, Workers' Liberty, were part of organising that. We saw it as a move to set up a coordination of local Momentum groups which would allow them to organise discussion and campaigning beyond the formal office-down structure, and would thus rally weight to force a democratisation of Momentum. The conference elected a committee, but essentially nothing came of it. Many local Momentum groups and activists were demoralised. The committee was fairly evenly divided between supporters of something like the perspective we advocated, and people who oriented to the defence of what we criticised as left antisemitism and who insisted that Momentum was "finished". Neither camp had the weight or the energy to make the new project fly on their course against the opposition of the other camp.

We continued to run candidates for NCG elections, to develop *The Clarion* magazine (launched in September 2016 as an effort to regroup the Momentum left), to participate in local Momentum groups, and to develop initiatives like Stop the Labour Purge, the Labour Campaign for Free Movement and (from December 2018) Labour for a Socialist Europe. Those initiatives had conferences, committees, and so on. With others they had a big impact on the left-wing Labour conference of September 2019. Labour for a Socialist Europe developed a few (but only a few) local groups, and was able to run a distinctive left Labour campaign-within-the-campaign in the December 2019 general election.

All those initiatives were unable to become more than small and loose networks. Labour for a Socialist Europe (L4SE), for obvious reasons, withered after Labour's December 2019 defeat and the 23 January 2020 parliamentary vote to push through Brexit, though its political work is carried on in a wider framework by Momentum Internationalists, launched by L4SE people in early 2020. Many of the other camp from Grassroots Momentum regrouped in the Labour Left Alliance in July 2019, with noticeably little impact at the left-wing Labour conference of September 2019.

Meanwhile, Momentum gained new (electronic) members from its (electronic) activity for the June 2017 general election — apps, messages, and so on, especially for mobilising people to work in marginals. By April 2018 it claimed 40,000 members. Momentum groups survived in some areas as local left caucuses without bothering too much about the national office. They dwindled in others. They were taken over by supporters of the national office in yet others. In Manchester they simply got out the numbers. In Lewisham, south London, in April 2018, a set of officers elected at an ad hoc meeting in a pub downstairs bar, by people mostly until then unknown to the active local Momentum group in which Workers' Liberty people worked harmoniously with a range of leftists, was instantly "recognised" by the Momentum office. Maybe

Labour for a Socialist Europe campaigned against Brexit and for workers' solidarity across borders.

some Momentum groups will now revive as lockdown eases in 2021-2. But for the peak years of the Corbyn era, 2017-2019, Momentum was a big "Labour left" which nevertheless fell short of even a minimal version of previous Labour lefts. It did, through its electronic communications, get the vote out for internal Labour Party elections (though for left slates decided opaquely and often with little left consensus). It did help Labour's public election efforts. But it allowed no political debate, it didn't help the left to advance in CLPs, and it played little role at Labour Party conferences, except in 2017 when it played the bad role of helping the leadership stop the conference debating Brexit. In Young Labour it played a bad role; in Labour Students, no role. In short, Momentum failed entirely in the tasks of a grassroots Labour left after September 2015; but it also had clout to pre-empt the space in which a better left might have developed.

And it became in some ways like 38 Degrees. Not in being a broad movement open to all comers, but in being an office-down, staff-heavy, almost-exclusively-electronic movement. To start its office, Jon Lansman chose young people with no or little previous labour movement background, such as James Schneider, one of its first "National Organisers", who had previously been an active Liberal Democrat. Schneider went on from Momentum to a job in the "Leader's Office", and now "does comms", as they say, for Yanis Varoufakis's "Progressive International". The other early "National Organisers", Emma Rees and Adam Klug, also had little labour background and also went on to other posts in the world of "doing comms". By the time of the July 2020 NCG election Momentum had 20 paid staff. In a conversation in the run-up to that election,

Jon Lansman told the writer that (to his dismay) "the office staff" (not himself) ran Momentum and should be held responsible for its shortcomings.

Schneider, Rees, and Klug, and dozens of others who circulated through jobs in the Momentum office, or in The World Transformed, or in the "Leader's Office", or in individual MPs' offices, were and are not malevolent, not Stalinist, not right-wing. But in previous labour movement left groupings, even the most unsatisfactory, the leading figures were people with a record and accessibility in the movement. They would be MPs, candidates, councillors, delegates at conferences and committees, people who came to meetings and could be heard and debated with. Now much went through people appointed as "comms" technicians and operating behind opaque office walls. The Blairite infection of Labour with the culture of the NGO and the quango continued in the Corbyn era, and even in its left and "grassroots" wing.

The pre-2015 Labour left

Part of the reason why that culture could dominate was that the active representatives of a more democratic, less "managerial" culture had become weak by 2015. The Campaign for Labour Party Democracy, a group dating back to the early 1970s, had kept plugging away through the Blair years. But its core was ageing and diminishing, and only slightly refreshed in the Corbyn years. It has a reserved seat in the Momentum NCG, and weight in the negotiations in the left about internal election slates. Its basic pitch through the Corbyn years was, even more than Momentum's, to support the Party leadership at all costs and through all twists and turns. At the September 2019 conference it ended up advising delegates to back the platform on all, absolutely all, issues, so as to "support the leadership" and give it no difficulties in the coming General Election. The Labour Representation Committee was the biggest other longstanding group of the Labour left in 2015. It had been launched in 2004 by John McDonnell MP, after some agitation by Workers' Liberty and others for a movement for "labour representation" to combat the Blair-Brown Labour leadership's shutting-down of space for working-class political voices. For some years it was relatively lively, driven by young activists like Owen Jones and Andrew Fisher employed in McDonnell's parliamentary office. By 2015 it had withered, with little activity outside its own annual conference and none of the detailed work in preparation for and at Labour Party conferences which CLPD still did. It did not revive in the Corbyn years. It ended them by joining the Labour Left Alliance mentioned above, critical of the Labour Party leadership mostly because of the leadership's haphazard attempts to signal distance from left antisemitism.

Socialist Appeal, the section of the old Militant group which had stayed in the Labour Party after that group split in 1992, had revived a bit from about 2010 by systematically setting up "Marxist Societies" on university campuses

Socialist Appeal: not much engaged.

with a regular routine of propagandist meetings. It was dedicated to the idea that impending economic crises will make "the masses move politically", and then "they will move through their traditional organisations", i.e. in Britain the Labour Party. The Marxists should be sitting there ready. While awaiting "the crisis", however, and even during the crises of 2008-9 and of Covid-slump, Socialist Appeal was not and is not much engaged in the Labour Party. It made no effort to intervene in Momentum when it was relatively open, in 2016. In 2016, around Jeremy Corbyn's second leadership election, several members of Socialist Appeal were among hundreds excluded from Labour in the same way as hundreds or thousands had been in 2015. Socialist Appeal showed no interest in working with the Stop the Labour Purge campaign or even, if they thought that campaign inadequate, in setting up a better one. Essentially they responded to the exclusions with a shrug.

The Socialist Workers' Party and the Socialist Party stayed outside the Labour Party in the Corbyn period, though here and there they attended a few meetings of Momentum in its earliest period. They could thus play a part in the battle to shape the Corbyn surge only by way of the influence of advocating ideas from outside. What they advocated was not helpful. Both presented themselves as the most eager supporters of Corbyn's politics, deploring only compromises which they saw Corbyn as being forced to make with established interests in the Labour Party. All moves by Corbyn and his team towards a more internationalist line on Brexit, or towards recognition of antisemitism as a problem, they censured as those evil compromises.

Workers' Liberty had been more active in Constituency Labour Parties than Socialist Appeal, especially since 2010, but we were few in numbers and those CLPs had been mostly unlively. We worked in and with Momentum for a more democratic and critical culture. We endeavoured to develop Young Labour and Labour Students, and the left within them; to build initiatives like Stop the Labour Purge, the Labour Campaign for Free Movement and Labour for a Socialist Europe. We did much useful work, but in the end we had not enough initial "critical mass" to counter the weight of the quasi-NGO, quasi-Stalinoid, office-down culture which dominated the Corbyn movement. That culture made the Corbyn movement unable to deal with two big issues which fragmented the left in 2016-2020 and contributed to Corbyn's demoralising defeat in December 2019: Brexit and antisemitism.

Brexit

In the run-up to the 23 June 2016 referendum, Brexit did not look like a difficult issue within Labour. We now know that Seamus Milne and Andrew Murray, key figures in Corbyn's inner circle, voted Leave on 23 June. They weren't saying that then. Almost the whole labour movement and left was united for a Remain vote. (Barring the *Morning Star*, *The Socialist*, and *Socialist Worker*; but *Socialist Worker* was visibly embarrassed about its Leave stance). The 1970s anti-EUism of the Labour left and the unions had been fading for decades, since Thatcherism and the "social Europe" talk of the late 1980s. The visit by EU Commission president Jacques Delors to the 1988 TUC Congress signalled a turning point. Jeremy Corbyn, like most of those previously educated in that 1970s anti-EUism, had long since (though, as we would see, with inner reservations) accepted that Brexit was in fact a right-wing project. After the fiasco of Labour's joint campaign with the Tories in the 2014 Scottish independence referendum, no-one on the Labour right disputed that Labour should make a distinct effort for Remain rather than merging into the Tory-dominated "official" Britain Stronger in Europe campaign.

Workers' Liberty had opposed anti-EUism since the 1960s, even when almost all others on the left were anti-EU. We worked to get a distinctly left-wing and working-class Remain voice in the campaign: an argument based on cross-border workers' unity to level up; on reducing borders especially to workers' free movement; and on the proposition that erecting new borders would only sharpen competitive capitalist pressures to entice investment to one side or another by reducing social overheads. That was difficult. We could win votes in Momentum for that idea, but not get Momentum to push it publicly. John McDonnell made some good speeches in the referendum campaign, but as an individual. We worked to build on the somewhat NGO-ish "Another Europe is Possible" campaign, which presented some of the ideas we wanted, though in an idiom of "progressive" cross-partyism (Greens, Plaid Cymru, Friends of the Earth, etc.)

Everyone's responses were shaped by the expectation that Remain would win, as the opinion polls indicated it would right up to 23 June, and that

Corbyn's Labour floundered on Brexit. Image: bit.ly/bil-con

would probably sideline the issue for years to come. Leave won. The Labour right seized on the shock to try to unseat Corbyn, with rolling shadow cabinet resignations and a vote of no-confidence in him by Labour MPs. They said that Corbyn had been weak in the referendum campaign. It was true, but the Labour right had been even weaker, though, in the person of Alan Johnson, it held the "franchise" to run Labour's independent effort. Corbyn saw out the challenge, retaining the support of the unions and winning a new leadership contest by a bigger margin than in 2015.

We now know that finding even a half-workable formula for Brexit within the (demagogically) vague parameters defined by the 2016 Leave campaign would take the Tories four and a half years after June 2016, and even after four and a half years the formula would be at best only half-workable. The rational response from Corbyn's Labour to the 23 June result should have been to point out that what Brexit meant was undefined, and that the narrow snap vote should not be taken to give the Tories a mandate for whatever formula they might cook up, still less to mandate Labour to support that yet-undefined formula. The issue should be reconsidered when the Tories had a formula to propose, and in the meantime Labour would continue a principled opposition to raising new barriers between countries. Jeremy Corbyn, however, responded on 24 June by calling on the Tories to activate "Article 50" (the formal opening of Brexit procedures) immediately. Corbyn would continue to defend free movement between Britain and the EU27 until November 2016, but with little support in Labour's top ranks (none from John McDonnell) and none from Momentum; he eventually collapsed on that issue too. The Tories quickly committed themselves to a "hard" version of Brexit, but would not activate "Article 50" until February 2017. When they did, Corbyn put a three-line whip to back the Tories. 47 Labour MPs voted against, and several shadow cabinet members, mostly from the left, resigned in order to vote against.

The best guess must be that Corbyn's advisers, their perceptions skewed by their own private pro-Brexit views, thought on 24 June 2016 that the Tories would be pushing through Brexit easily and soon. Their perceptions further skewed by a manipulative and catchpenny philosophy of politics, Corbyn's advisers thought that a Labour "do it now" declaration on 24 June would be clever politics. Labour would both be seen as accepting the "will of the people", and able soon to make gains by showing the bad results of the Tories' Brexit. In fact they were condemning Corbyn Labour to years of torment in which its sense of principle and its credibility would be destroyed by successive contortions. Labour would try to run on the claim that they could negotiate a good Brexit, while the Tories lacked that negotiating skill. Labour would vote for a Brexit deal, but only one which met vague and incoherent "tests". Then, in the end, in December 2020, Labour under Keir Starmer voted for Boris Johnson's "deal", manifestly meeting none of the "tests", with little protest from Corbynites, though Corbyn himself abstained. Labour opposed a second referendum; and then, under pressure from the Labour base and an electorate increasingly disillusioned with Brexit, it edged towards being for it, but only in certain forms and under certain conditions never clearly defined and never met. All working-class, socialist, and internationalist principle was abandoned, and yet pro-Brexit voters would still see Labour as quibbling.

Some argue that Labour had no choice but to back Brexit after June 2016, and it was its failure to do so that lost it the December 2019 election. About a third of Labour voters had voted Leave on 23 June 2016. But around the same proportion of Scottish National Party voters had gone for Leave. The SNP kept its opposition to Brexit, and didn't lose votes, mostly because those pro-Leave voters thought other issues which rallied them to the SNP more important. Labour could have done similar, and convinced many in the pro-Brexit minority of its base on the Brexit issue too, but only by keeping up a sharp agitation on cuts, the NHS, and social provision through the whole period. It didn't. By its equivocation Labour only made voters see it as... equivocating. The June 2017 general election was a partial but instructive exception. Then, Labour's manifesto accepted Brexit, but in the small print. Most voters saw Labour as anti-Brexit, or at least softer-Brexit. The strong anti-cuts message pulled them to Labour against a Tory party calling for a "strong and stable" majority precisely so that (it hoped) it would be well-placed to do Brexit.

Corbyn Labour's failure on Brexit destroyed its claim to represent new principle and consistency in politics. It was also a failure of hopes for party democracy. At all the decisive points after 23 June 2016, policies were handed down from above, rather than being democratically discussed with and decided by the always anti-Brexit party membership. The leadership kept Brexit off the agenda of both 2016 and 2017 conferences (with the active help of Momentum in 2017). By the 2018 conference it could no longer keep Brexit off the agenda. It engineered a single, fudged, composite motion to come to conference floor so that there would be no debate. (Some of the anti-Brexit left at the time adopted a "hopeful" reading of the fudge to claim it as a victory. As they came to recognise later, sometimes much later, it wasn't. Workers' Liberty people at conference were for the moment swept along by the "hopeful" mood, but one of us had been the last hold-out in the compositing meeting against the "one motion" ploy, and we soon recovered our balance).

The Brexit "debate" pushed back all possibilities for the new Labour Party membership to re-educate itself and to equip itself to go out and educate and win over others, in workplaces and in neighbourhoods. It put a lid on the hopeful possibilities of 2015 on several fronts: on the opening out of party democracy, on the re-education of a new contingent of activists, on offering the wider electorate an honest politics of principle in place of manipulation and soft-soaping.

Antisemitism

That antisemitism would befoul the Corbyn era, both in reality and in the electorate's perception of it, was also unpredictable, but maybe not as unpredictable as with Brexit. As of 2015, Workers' Liberty had been arguing for some 30 years that the left had become tainted by antisemitism. Much far-left thinking on Israel — the world's only majority-Jewish state, whose history is inextricably bound up with the history of antisemitism — had been shaped by an "absolute anti-Zionist" perspective that insisted the Israeli Jews should be denied national self-determination. For the sake of supposed "anti-imperialism", Israel should be replaced by an Arab or Islamic state "from the river to the sea", and the Jews would have to flee or accept subject status. That had its roots in the view of world politics as a matter of "two camps", "imperialism" (meaning the USA and its allies) and "revolution" (meaning the USA's opponents, however imperialistic) propagated by Stalinism and by a wider "Third-Worldist" left in the 1960s and 70s. We defended the traditional (pre-Stalinist) socialist approach to national oppression, which today impels solidarity with the Palestinians and support for equality between Palestinian Arabs and Israeli Jews — including equal national rights, "two nations, two states". That the "absolute anti-Zionist" line was utterly unreal as a practical programme — useless to win redress for the Palestinians in the real world — did not diminish its noxiousness as a preconceived attitude to the only compact Jewish population in the world, and to the Jews worldwide ("Zionists") who, by inescapable shapings of history, felt affinity and sympathy with that population.

The "absolute anti-Zionists" did not think themselves antisemitic. On the contrary, they considered themselves the most virtuous anti-racists. Israel not only had racist policies (as more or less every existing state does). It was in essence and inescapably a "racist state". Its crushing even by Islamist clerical-fascists like Hamas, or like Iran's rulers, would thus be anti-racist. This "political antisemitism" was distinct from the old-fashioned "biological" antisemitism of the right, which abhorred all Jews because of supposed inherited traits. The "political antisemites" of the left would defend synagogues against attacks by neo-Nazis; they would feel no necessary personal animosity to individual Jews; they might even be proud of being Jewish themselves. They would claim that their hostility to "Zionists" was not to an identity imprinted on most Jews by history, but only to a particular political choice.

In the 1970s the "abolish Israel" programme had been expressed, on the left, in hopeful but naive terms: there should be a secular democratic state in all the territory of British-Mandate Palestine, uniting Israeli Jews and Palestinian Arabs as one people. (But how? Free unity is possible only if it is voluntary on both sides. How of all the world's neighbouring peoples can those two, at war on and off for decades, insecure in their national rights, be the first to think the right to self-rule now superfluous? The first to have high assurance that friendly merger would give them all they wanted?)

Long before 2015, the naive hope had begun to curdle. Talk of a secular democratic state faded in favour of root-and-branch denunciation of Israel, usually with no positive alternative expressed, but usually also with the implication that no progress could be achieved as long as anything at all like Israel survived, and that anything Hamas or Hezbollah might do against Israel was justified. Those who dropped the "secular democratic state" slogan generally continued their opposition to a "two states" policy. If pressed, they would sometimes say their answer was socialism in the entire region.

The *Morning Star* remained, on paper, for "two states". But the Communist Party of Britain agitated vehemently for boycotting Israel. The *Morning Star* declared that there was little point protesting about antisemitism "until its root cause — Israel's criminal behaviour — is dealt with". The paper eventually apologised for that declaration, but its tone continued to inform the coverage. If "two states" was in the small print, the suggestion was more that this was a concession which might be allowed if Israel mended its ways improbably well, rather than that it was the only way to recognise the democratic self-determination of both peoples, Palestinian and Israeli-Jewish. The *Morning Star* loudly supported the "right of return", meaning the right for maybe seven million grandchildren and other descendants of 1948 refugees collectively to repossess the territory which is now Israel: a demand different from individual freedom of movement, and incompatible with "two states".

Jeremy Corbyn in 2015 was a longstanding *Morning Star* columnist. He was

"Absolute anti-Zionism" nourished antisemitism. Image: bit.ly/az-as

also a longstanding associate of people around the Stop The War Coalition who plainly supported wiping out Israel. He had supported Palestinian rights as an MP, but no more vocally than others such as Emily Thornberry and Lisa Nandy who had stated support for the right of Israel to exist and criticism of Hamas. Corbyn supported the "right of return", but marginally and without apparent understanding of its conflict with the support he also expressed, more loudly, for "two states". He opposed boycotting Israel. He must have known he was differentiating from the *Morning Star*. Maybe, having paid much attention in the decades before 2015 to Latin America, he was influenced by Cuba's rapprochement with Israel: I don't know. In October 2014 Ed Miliband, as Labour leader, whipped Labour MPs to support a symbolic Commons vote to recognise Palestine as a state. The Tories mostly abstained. The Jewish Board of Deputies complained, but the row was small. No Labour MP voted against. (Jeremy Corbyn, oddly, acted as teller for the mostly Tory and DUP MPs voting against, but that was presumably some parliamentary technicality). In June 2020, after Corbyn was ousted, the new foreign secretary, Lisa Nandy, called for Britain to ban imports of West Bank settlement products if Israel annexed the West Bank, or large parts of it. In the Corbyn era, however, for example in the 2017 and 2019 Labour manifestos, there was no significant shift in Labour policy on Israel-Palestine. It remained a policy for "two states" but with little or no active solidarity to help achieve that.

The outcry against antisemitism in Labour under Corbyn was not an attempt to deflect or discredit some more energetic solidarity with Palestinian rights. It was not, as the *Morning Star* claimed it was, a ploy "to prevent a rare parliamentary champion of the rights of the Palestinian people from achieving the highest political office in Britain" (9 April 2019). It was not even an addled argument about the policy of a general boycott of Israel and its antisemitic implications. In autumn 2015, Luke Akehurst, a pro-Israel doyen of the Labour right, expressed worry about a vote on boycotting Israel being brought to Labour conference (where it might pass thanks to Unite and Unison union policy). He estimated that Corbyn and his team would probably avoid that. Which they did, and with little trouble.

The outcry was about what it said on the tin: antisemitism. Shadow Chancellor John McDonnell had a worse back-story on the issue than Corbyn: in 1985 he was briefly editor of *Labour Herald*, a paper launched by the rancidly-antisemitic Workers' Revolutionary Party of Gerry Healy with Ken Livingstone and Ted Knight as initial front-men. McDonnell, however, had re-thought and re-learned. He said of the outcry on antisemitism: "It isn't a smear campaign... I've seen the evidence" (6 February 2019). Those making the outcry sometimes exaggerated, and some of them had other reasons to pick up anything that discredited Corbyn. That was utterly secondary to "the evidence" of substance.

April 2016 and Ken Livingstone

The row was only a muttering until April 2016, when Ken Livingstone got himself suspended from Labour. Someone had dug out an old social media post from Naz Shah, Labour MP for Bradford West, reproducing an image saying that the "solution for the Israel-Palestine conflict" was for Israel to be "relocated" into the USA: a coded form of "drive the Jews out", with the assumption that once they were driven out the USA would let them in (unlike in the 1930s or 40s). Shah quickly apologised and remains an MP. But Ken Livingstone approached the media to offer comment. He said that Shah had done nothing wrong. He asserted, as if that proved his case, that Hitler had "supported Zionism". (This was a garbled version of the story of a deal which the Jewish community in Palestine made with the Nazis to enable some Jews to escape from Germany to Palestine with some of their property). And he refused to retract or apologise.

Livingstone's declarations had no connection at all with supporting Palestinian rights. The same would be true of practically all the antisemitic comments which circulated in and around Corbyn Labour, and which caused outcry. Many or most of them, in fact, would not be "smash Israel"-type anti-Zionism, but straight "old-fashioned" antisemitism, "Rothschild conspiracy", "Jewish power", stuff. Corbyn's own moralistic, rather than structural, critique of capitalism, and his leadership's use of populist concepts like "the rigged economy" — implying a conspiracy of nefarious "rigging" by evil people "behind the scenes", rather than explaining capitalism as a structure of class exploitation, within which we have power as members of the working class — left Corbynism ill-equipped to combat eruptions of these primitive, would-be "anti-finance" and "anti-capitalist" forms of antisemitism.

These were given fertile soil, and accompanied, by the "political" antisemitism, or "absolute anti-Zionism", which people like Livingstone had carried for decades. To get from that to more "old-fashioned" antisemitism you had only to shift the labels in the conspiracy-theory frame, to name the villain as "Jewish financiers" or "Rothschild bankers" rather than Israel, the "lobby", and "Zionism". Livingstone had from end-1981 to 1985 worked closely with Gerry Healy's "Workers' Revolutionary Party", which by then was in the pay of the Iraqi and Libyan regimes. It denounced *Socialist Organiser*, a forerunner of *Solidarity* and Workers' Liberty, as part of a worldwide "Zionist connection" (with Reagan, Thatcher, etc.) because we reported on its financial connections. Livingstone remained close to Healy after the WRP blew up in scandal. In 1994, he wrote a laudatory introduction to a laudatory biography of Healy. By then, despite his residual sympathy for Healy-type "revolutionism", the once-left Livingstone had become on most issues a middle-of-the-road Labour careerist. He ran as an independent for Mayor of London in 2000, after narrowly losing a rigged selection, and won. Blair readmitted Livingstone to the Labour Party in time for the 2004 mayoral election, and Livingstone served as Labour mayor in 2004-8. He was suspended from office for a month in February 2006 by a legal panel because of antisemitic jibes against a Jewish journalist in February 2005. At an appeal hearing in October 2006 the judge found the suspension invalid on procedural grounds, though Livingstone's jibes "offensive" and "indefensible". Livingstone lost to the Tories in 2008 and in 2012, and then indicated he was retiring from front-line politics.

In November 2015 Corbyn brought the elderly Livingstone back to "co-convene" Labour's "defence policy review" with pro-Trident shadow minister Maria Eagle. Why, I'm not clear: Corbyn's team had evidently already decided that challenging Labour's policy for Trident replacement was too hard. Anyway, Corbyn brought Livingstone back on the scene; and then Livingstone pushed himself forward to be the high-profile Labour defender of the Facebook post which Shah herself called indefensible.

It was Livingstone who took the initiative to blow up the antisemitism row, not an anti-Corbynite. Arbitrary exclusions of left-wingers were running high at the time, as they did from summer 2015 until after the 2016 Labour leadership election, but those were exclusions for having associated with left-wing groups, with no reference to antisemitism. Why Livingstone did it, we don't know. As we wrote at the time: "He is a Livingstone-serving opportunist, not a principled politician who will stand by his version of the truth, irrespective of consequences... He knows perfectly well that he is helping the Labour right and the Tories, sabotaging Labour's election campaign [for the May 2016 local elections]. He wants to do that? Why? The explanation may lie in Livingstone's dual character. Inside this supremely self-centred, manipulative politician Dr Jekyll-Livingstone there is imprisoned a contrary, irrational, egotist, Mr Hyde-Livingstone, who sometimes takes over". Who knows? Labour suspended Livingstone. He complained, protested, but eventually subsided or lost the attention of the media. He resigned from the Labour Party in 2018, before his case reached a Labour disciplinary tribunal.

Corbyn went along with the suspension of Livingstone, but made no substantive comment on what Livingstone had said. "There's no crisis... Where there is any racism in the party it will be dealt with and rooted out. I have been an anti-racist campaigner all my life... There is not a problem [with antisemitism]. We are totally opposed to antisemitism in any form within the party. The very small number of cases that have been brought to our attention have been dealt with swiftly and immediately, and they will be". That response would feed and define the downward spiral of the next four and a half years. More and more social media posts, expressing often the crudest antisemitism, would circulate. Some Labour activists, like Jackie Walker, would "do a Livingstone", gratuitously seeking media attention for comments which, at the very least, they knew to be offensive to Jewish Labour members (and which could serve no conceivable Palestinian-solidarity purpose). There would be "real-life" overspill, even if often in the indirect form where Jewish members complaining about antisemitism would instantly find themselves denounced as agents of a right-wing stitch-up. Some of it would target individual Jewish members, such as Luciana Berger, not a left-winger but initially, in September 2015, a prominent Corbyn ally, appointed by him with much fanfare as the first-ever front-bench spokesperson on mental health. Berger eventually quit Labour, in February 2019, and after a short spell with the feeble "Change UK" splinter group, joined the Lib Dems. As the row swirled on and on, Corbyn would still say that there was no problem, or if there was one, it was just that Labour's growth was statistically certain to draw in the odd bad apple. He himself had been "an anti-racist all his life". Ergo, no real problem. He was unable, or more likely unwilling, to recognise that some of the "political antisemites" considered themselves the best anti-racists and anti-fascists; that, in fact, they thought their reflex hostility to reflexly-Israel-empathising Jews was a sign of anti-racist virtue, because they identified "Zionists" as ipso facto the world's most potent racists. In March 2018 Corbyn put himself centre-stage, when he responded to the discovery of an old Facebook post in which he had objected to the taking-down (by Tower Hamlets council, led by an ex-left-Labour soft-Islamist!) of an antisemitic mural by saying evasively that "I sincerely regret that I did not look more closely at the image I was commenting on". (Note: regret. Not apologise).

Later in 2018, Corbyn and his office ran a long rearguard action to try to stop Labour's National Executive adopting the International Holocaust

Remembrance Alliance text on antisemitism, and in particular the clause indicating that in some circumstances it is antisemitic to "claim that the existence of a State of Israel is a racist endeavour". The text licenses criticism of Israel (as of any other state) for racist policies; it censures only claims that the very existence, in whatever form, with whatever policy changes, of any Israeli state, is in and of itself "racist". First Labour adopted a code based on the IHRA text but pointedly omitting that clause. Then, when the full text was pushed through, Corbyn's office still, unsuccessfully, sought a garbled "qualification" that would deem it not "antisemitic to describe Israel, its policies or the circumstances around its foundation as racist". (Racist "circumstances"?) At no point did Corbyn or his office confront the culture of left antisemitism which had washed into Labour with many of the "returners", explain what was wrong with it, promote debate and education. As Dave Rich of the Jewish community charity CST put it to *Solidarity*, "all we hear is: it's just 0.1% of the membership, and we'll discipline them and throw them out..." Corbyn was always walking backwards, forced to concede one concern after another about antisemitism but always grudgingly, reluctantly, and to the smallest extent he could get away with. By November 2019 a poll would find 44% of people thinking the Chief Rabbi right to comment on the 2019 election with worries about Labour being antisemitic, and only 27% thinking him wrong. Some in Corbyn's Shadow Cabinet did better, notably John McDonnell and Emily Thornberry. But they never did enough, or gained enough weight, to offset Corbyn's evasions. And most of the left was unwilling to criticise Corbyn.

Corbyn himself was unwilling or unable to think through the issues. His office staff was dominated by people like Seamus Milne and Andrew Murray who were aligned with the *Morning Star*'s demonisation of Israel, and whose standard response to all political problems was to manage and manipulate them rather than seeking honest debate. According to the journalistic investigators Gabriel Pogrund and Patrick Maguire, even at times when the office staff, for reasons of ordinary prudence, would have favoured simple apologies, Corbyn was swayed by long-term associates from the 1970s and 1980s generation. These were not "returners" in the full sense of people who had been out of politics completely in the interim; rather, people who had been radicals or revolutionaries in the 1970s or 80s, settled down for decades to low-key Labour Party activity (signalled to themselves as still radical by such stances as against Israel), and then felt themselves on a winner again after 2015. In any case, the standard limiting factors of the Corbyn era — the failure to draw in young activists, the shortage of debate and education, the focus on hopes of "Corbyn for PM" rather than rebuilding in class struggle, and the influence of *Morning Star* type politics — were allowed to have deadly effect.

Curbs on debate, curbs on development

In 2019, Ken Livingstone at first agreed to debate Workers' Liberty at our summer school on Zionism and antisemitism. I don't know why, but he confirmed, and re-confirmed. A few weeks before the event, and unsurprisingly to us, he withdrew, pleading domestic difficulties and saying anyway he was "retired from politics". We approached seven different people from the "absolute anti-Zionist" left to take the speaking slot. They didn't have to identify with Livingstone, only to take the chance to criticise our views in front of our loosest friends and associates. All refused. Throughout the whole Corbyn era, our repeated attempts to get debates on the issue, in our own Workers' Liberty meetings or as sponsored by local Labour Parties or Momentum groups, produced only one or two results. Generally, the "absolute anti-Zionists" would not debate, rather than sniping on social media.

In July 2018, with the help of Another Europe Is Possible, we were able to generate a face-to-face debate on Brexit, Grace Blakeley vs Michael Chessum. In 2019 Paul Embery debated Ruth Cashman on Brexit at our summer school, Ideas for Freedom. Few other debates were set up. Twice, for example, we got agreement from Aaron Bastani, prominent in Labour circles through his work in Novara Media, to debate us on Brexit: once he withdrew a few hours before the meeting, the other time he just didn't turn up.

Given that the previous twenty years had been the era of Blair, Brown, and Cameron, and with only sporadic resistance, it was inescapable that the Labour left reassembled in 2015 would be politically unformed, chaotic, and burdened with much dross. Discussion, debate, polemic, education could have changed that quickly. Despite Momentum saying that The World Transformed would provide just that, there was very little basic debate.

From the top, Labour politics in the Corbyn era was still largely "managed", as it had been in the Blair era. Nearer the base, polemic and debate was largely displaced by social-media "flaming". The *Morning Star* published an article (26 July 2019) with the shape of an actual polemic against Workers' Liberty, over our efforts in the Free Our Unions campaign. (It argued that the campaign was too "absolutist" in its push for repealing all anti-strike laws; that it distracted unnecessarily from other campaigns; and that the involvement of an allegedly "minuscule political sectlet", i.e. Workers' Liberty, made the campaign insufficiently "broad-based").

Apart from that *Morning Star* article, polemical comment within the Labour left in the Corbyn era mostly took the form not of articles and arguments but of social-media snippets "exposing" this or that group, or this or that person, on the grounds of this or that phrase extracted from context and branded "racist", or whatever. As we commented, "discussion of language can and frequently does displace discussion of things and ideas". Consideration of the substantive argument in an article, for example, would be pushed aside in favour of anathematising the choice of words in some selected sentence.

There was much criticism of antisemitism which was perforce of odd sentences and small passages, because the antisemitism was most expressed in social-media snippets rather than anything long-form. Often even justified criticism included little effort to explain *why* the snippet was antisemitic. It was just an "exposure". It elicited not counter-argument and debate but instead such responses as "I retweeted such-and-such without reading it carefully, and you're targeting me just to serve Israeli interests". In that area, careful long-form explanations were circulated. We circulated three pamphlets: *Left Anti-Semitism*; *Two Nations Two States*; and *Arabs, Jews, and Socialism*. Dave Rich and Dave Hirsh published books (*The Left's Jewish Problem*; *Contemporary Left Antisemitism*) with explanations. Steve Cohen's *That's Funny, You Don't Look Antisemitic* was republished. There was little attempt at long-form reply. Generally, polemic, even unsound polemic like the *Morning Star*'s referred to above, was displaced in the culture of the left by a fever of social-media "flaming".

Thomas Carlyle called the French Revolution of 1789-93 a "Whirlpool of Words". Leon Trotsky wrote that "revolutions are always verbose", and showed that the run-up to the Russian Revolution of October 1917 was days full of intense meetings, discussions, debates, and not in fact barricades or even strikes. France's May 1968 is known for its "Night of the Barricades", but much more of it was about innumerable meetings and arguments in workplace and campus occupations, in Action Committees, and day to day on the streets.

The Corbyn surge was always going to be tamer than those great events. Its Whirlpool of Words was, however, not only smaller. It had its tone set by the off-hand tweet more than the speech or article coming as part of a debate, even of an ill-tempered or flawed debate.

Corbyning Alone?

Social, technological, and cultural shifts have probably created new obstacles to organising left-wing young people, as well as creating new facilities useful for that organising. The failure to overcome those obstacles in the Corbyn era was a failure of the left, and not inevitable.

Robert Putnam's book *Bowling Alone* (first edition 2000, second edition 2020) is justly criticised for its description of social connectedness as social "capital", an analogue of business capital and human "capital", and for its soupy liberal advocacy of general "togetherness". It also gives extensive factual documentation, difficult to dismiss. No research comparable to Putnam's has been done in Britain, but many partial inquiries and observations suggest that the trends of declining social connectedness as in the USA have also prevailed in Britain. The historical timing is surely different — union density started declining in the USA from the mid-1950s, and rose in Britain until 1979 — but probably much of what Putnam has documented in the USA has also happened in Britain, only later.

Putnam gives some weight in social atomisation to technology, for example the rise of television (which still commands an average of three hours a day from people in the UK, more in fact than in the USA) and of the internet and social media. For the first time in history, those technologies offer well-produced entertainment, and even a sort of ersatz togetherness, which can be consumed individually, without meeting up, each person at their own screen. Up to the 1970s, even, Labour youth groups in Britain would draw in many people by social activities (gigs, hikes, card-playing, whatever), and surely they were helped by the fact that alternative recreation was scant and often expensive.

Putnam explicitly rejects technological determinism, and mentions increased economic inequality as a driver. Other strands of neoliberalism, such as increased economic insecurity, are probably also drivers. So are the defeats of the working-class movement over recent decades. Increased economic inequality and insecurity may boost organisation and solidarity if they are continuously combatted, but not if the working-class organisations fighting them are caught in a pattern of "damage limitation" and retreat.

Putnam records the facts. "The same phenomenon — observing up, doing down — appears in [many] spheres of American life... By many measures 'doing' culture (as opposed to merely consuming it) has been declining... We certainly have not lost our taste for listening to music... but fewer and fewer of us play together".

In politics: "Less and less party activity involves volunteer collaboration among committed partisans. More and more involves the skilled (and expensive) techniques of effective mass marketing... The wherewithal for mass marketing... has steadily replaced... grassroots citizen networks as the coin of the realm".

Union membership numbers have declined, and: "the type of involvement in unions has slackened. Unions are now seen mostly as hired bargaining agents, not as a social movement".

Political agitation and contestation has not diminished. Rather, we have seen "the 'bureaucratisation of social discontent', by mass promotion campaigns, by full-time employees whose professional careers are defined in terms of social movement participation..." Membership of associations of one sort or another in the USA has *increased*, not decreased, but the form of the association has changed. "In the last third of the [20th] century... mailing list membership has continued to expand, with the creation of an entirely new species of 'tertiary' association whose members never actually meet. At the same time, active involvement in face-to-face organisations has plummeted". Putnam notes that in the USA the plummet, the disproportion between mailing-list support and face-to-face activism, has affected the left more than the right, which has retained bases of week-to-week, face-to-face organising in the churches even despite the decline in church attendance.

Those trends have so far been sharpened rather than reversed by the rise of the internet and social media, as Putnam finds in his 2020 Afterword. "The Internet and especially Twitter are the worst places [for real discussion] because you don't have relationships and people are trying to show how smart they are. They're trying to show how devoted they are to their team. So the kind of political engagement, the kind of public square, that we get from social media, is generally terrible".

Jean Twenge has suggested that the rise of social media goes with teenagers (even pre-pandemic) spending more time at home, less time out socialising, than previous generations. Putnam concurs: "Starting about 2011-2, rapid growth in teen use of smartphones and social media coincided with... a significant decline in in-person social interactions, such as getting together with friends". That is plausibly a factor in the marked rise of depression and anxiety among teenagers in Britain and the USA. And what happens in our teens, generally the most "social" part of our lives, feeds through into later life.

"When volunteers are asked how they happened to get involved in their particular activity, the most common answer is, 'someone asked me'." Only, too many of the activists have become "comms professionals", oriented towards broadcast electronic communication rather than the sort of conversations where one person explains an activity to another and asks them individually to volunteer.

Many of the limited number of "Corbynite" youth activated around 2015 drifted towards bureaucratic machine politics, and often seeing politics as a matter of a career in the world of NGOs, think-tanks, "comms" operations, MPs' offices, or union officialdom. At least one factor there must be that they had grown up, in their teens, with that sort of NGO-type activity as the visible model of leftish politics. Their drift, in turn, diverted them from building week-by-week active youth groups in the constituencies and on the campuses; and thus blocked the emergence of a different model.

I commented above on the Corbyn period seeing a decline, rather than a rise, in street demonstrations, at least if you take out the big anti-Brexit demonstrations which Corbyn Labour did not support. Putnam's documentation tells us, also, that when there are big street protests, the link with continuous week-by-week political activity has become looser, or at least one requiring more work.

"Demonstrations and other public protests in Washington have become somewhat larger and more frequent since the late 1960s... On the other hand, the great civil rights and Vietnam marches of the sixties were preceded and followed by continuing activism in communities across the country, whereas a 'March on Washington' in the 1990s provided no assurance of continuing, community-based action".

In Britain, the famous nuclear-disarmament and Vietnam protests of the 1960s were in fact modest by today's standards. The Vietnam protests of March and October 1968 are estimated by some at 100,000, by others as few as 30,000. But those who joined the demonstrations would also join local meetings and activities of Campaign for Nuclear Disarmament groups, Vietnam Solidarity Campaign groups, Labour youth groups, student Labour Clubs or other groups, trade unions... That is why those protests go down in history as nodes of a revival of left activism which flowed on for years, in thousands of meetings, arguments, debates, neighbourhood activities, workplace activities as well as the dozens of big demonstrations. The sort of activism mediated through week-by-week meetings, with debates and arguments, and the sort of activism shown by the demonstrations, intertwined closely. Of course, many back then came to only the occasional demonstration and the occasional meeting, and then drifted away. We had "flakiness" in truckloads. We didn't have a disconnect: big street protests, or big spates of multiple protests, as with BLM in summer 2020 or Kill The (Police) Bill in spring 2021, with comparatively very little week-to-week local-group activity preceding or following them. Or, the converse, people who consider themselves "activists" and follow electronic-messaging circles or even attend meetings keenly, but routinely don't attend the street protests. In the Corbyn period, when Momentum endorsed a street demonstration, which it did from time to time, noticeably few people identifiable as "Momentum activists" would turn out. And so the next twist of the disconnect: the new demonstration-goer would not be able to see Momentum or the Labour Party as a good way to "stay involved".

Technology surely plays a role here. With the internet and smartphones, much greater numbers can be informed quickly about protests than in the days when you could find out about a protest only by seeing a poster or someone personally handing you a leaflet. So, if you want to find out about further protests, just follow the same electronic messaging to be "involved". No need to join a group or attend meetings. Some people can perceive just following and transmitting electronic messages, signing appeals online, and so on as "political activism", even if they do little in-person. Output filtered by electronic messaging can seem sufficient; so can input filtered by electronic messaging. In the 1980s, or earlier, even dilatory left-wing activists would regularly read one of the heavier bourgeois newspapers. They exposed themselves daily

Big street protests, but a looser link with week-to-week activism.

to information (of which those newspapers carry a lot) and to bourgeois arguments, and had to learn to read between the lines of the information and unpick the arguments. Even the dilatory discussed and argued daily with workmates or fellow-students of differing views. With their window to the world around them and to the left in particular given by smartphones and social media (more exactly: by the electronic messages they choose to pick up, since most people don't read most messages), instead of serious newspapers and in-person conversations and meetings, people become more connected, in a way. They also become more disconnected, in another way. They may feel "involved" or even swamped, almost every minute, but actually be left more atomised than seemingly less-connected activists geared to a week-by-week flow of in-person politics.

We will fate ourselves to disappointment if we expect a long-running surge of organised local-group activism (with meetings, debates, and so on) to flow automatically from the great Black Lives Matter demonstrations of 2020, or the student climate strikes of 2019, or the protests against the Police Bill in 2021. We can see one reason why the Corbyn moment of 2015 had easier success in transforming diffuse occasional-demonstration stirrings into week-by-week activism among older people who had assimilated the model of week-by-week in-person activism in their younger formative years, and it was harder with young people.

Technological determinism is out of place, though. From the Sanders movement in the USA since 2015, for all its weaknesses and the heavy NGO-y "comms professionals" element in it, some socialists have been able to extract a rise in week-to-week meeting-based activism of young people. Given a sufficient core of initial activists, with sufficient energy, oriented to building week-to-week activism and debate, resolved to use e-communication as a complement rather than a substitute, it can be done.

Lenin once commented that trade union organisation was sure to develop organically. Only, if the consciousness of priests shaped it, it would be Catholic social-partnership trade unionism, and if the consciousness of Marxists, then class-struggle trade unionism. Perhaps today we have to add another alternative. Social discontent among young people is sure to develop. Big street protests, even. Only, if the consciousness of people oriented to Stalinist-influenced, or NGO-y, or "comms professional" models of politics shapes it, then it will remain diffuse and sporadic. It requires the conscious activity of a sufficiently large and energetic body of class-struggle socialists to shape, from the mass of discontent, a stream of activism based in meetings and discussions which will then flow on, over years, into lively workplace and neighbourhood organisations which can equip workers for effective class struggle.

Those class-struggle socialists need to use well the extra resources given to them by the internet and social media. As a complement. They are bound to fail if they rely on those resources to substitute for in-person activism and outreach, if they think that organised week-to-week in-person activism, meetings, debates and so on have become "old-fashioned" and no longer necessary. There may be an analogy here with the finding of social scientists about individual friendship. People who have and meet many "real-life" friends generally improve those friendships by adding social-media communication. People who use social media as a full-on substitute for "real-life" friends generally end up lonelier and more distressed.

The US political scientist Eitan Hersh is a conservative Democrat who criticises most Democrats as too left-wing. But some of his observations about US politics are instructive for understanding the role of social media in the failures of the Corbyn era. Even in the era of Obama's election victories and the Sanders movement, Hersh argues, right-wing Republicans in the USA do more in-person politics, "in the gun clubs and the churches", than the left broadly defined. Right-wing social media can then consolidate people in a web of conspiracy theories. When the left (broadly defined) relies on social media, that doesn't work well, says Hersh, because "online politics is all about provocation and signalling outrage. But changing people's minds... requires empathy and face-to-face engagement". And, he could add, consolidating changed minds into a stable and workable socialist politics requires long-form discussion and debate, by word of mouth and in writing, something more than the mish-mashes of conspiracy theories which can serve to consolidate people in right-wing politics.

"We used to think more about grassroots organising focused on unions, for example", writes Hersh, "but unions have collapsed while churches have gotten disproportionately Republican". Too many US leftists, says Hersh, fool themselves that they're politically effective when in fact they are "political hobbyists", part of a froth of "consultant-driven activism". They may do a lot of "signing online petitions", and "many of us think we're politically active — but in fact, we're doing little more than signalling who we are to other people" in a fairly small circle. "It's not harder to go to a community meeting once a week today than it was 30 years ago, but it feels harder relative to the alternative".

Many Corbyn supporters participated only or mostly through social media. Social media have not made long-form discussion impossible or even unattractive. In fact, social media can amplify long-form events through the facility they give for advertising them more widely. The World Transformed estimated 5,000 people at their 2016 fringe festival at the Labour Party conference, many of them coming to Liverpool not for the conference but just for the fringe, and says that later years had bigger numbers. But social media do create a "soft" alternative to full political engagement, where, as Hersh put it, "many of us think we're politically active, but in fact, we're doing little more than signalling". To help people get past that and find ways into a surge of regular week-by-week activism, capable of spreading out through neighbourhoods and workplaces, requires energy, initiative, and drive from already-organised people. The Corbyn "Leader's Office", and too much of the top layer of the Corbyn surge, failed on that, not from idleness, but because of their political ideas, which made the "getting past" seem not so important to them. They thought of politics as something to be managed and manipulated, and a place to make careers in "comms", rather as something to be studied and debated.

Protesting too much?

Many "Corbynites" thought, and think, the effort by Workers' Liberty to develop a coherent organisation, week-by-week active on all fronts of the class struggle, intent on debate and education, and with explicit socialist-revolutionary aims, to be "sectarian" or even "cultish".

By some of the self-appointed ideological "border guards" of Corbynism, that thought was expressed in Stalinist-level denunciations and smears, almost all carried on social media, and often anonymously. A thoughtful argument against our approach was, however, developed and deserves an answer.

The *Chartist* magazine acknowledges that it "began its early days in the 1970s as a Trotskyist tendency". It is still on the left. It backed Corbyn in the 2015 and 2016 leadership contests. It has been better than most of the Labour left on Brexit and on antisemitism, and more critical of Corbyn. Thus when, in a book review by its editor, Mike Davis, in its April 2019 issue, it stated the case for the left to limit its focus to getting Corbyn and McDonnell into office, we must take it as deserving reply.

"Ultimately", wrote Davis, the weakness of Trotskyism "is the obsession with the October Revolution, and the quest to transplant the early Bolshevik template to forge revolution in a country, indeed a western world, that has long democratic traditions and entrenched institutions within a globalised capitalist system. What's the point of building an independent revolutionary party if many Trotskyist policies and demands can be achieved through the medium of a radical left party, particularly today with Labour led by Corbyn and McDonnell?" If we could get enough, or much, of what we wanted by levering Corbyn and McDonnell into office, then surely it would be a weakness to aim for a more laborious route? A central issue here is whether "many" or enough "Trotskyist policies" could in fact be won by pushing along Corbyn and McDonnell. First we need to unpick Davis's idea of the more laborious route to be avoided, that of building an "independent revolutionary party".

The main forerunner of the Communist Party in its Marxist early years was the British Socialist Party, which was affiliated to the Labour Party. The Communist Party itself sought affiliation. The general rule for Trotskyists since then has been to participate in the Labour Party, using exactly the same rights given by its relatively open structure as exercised by other political groupings in Labour, Progress, the Fabian Society, Momentum, whatever. We do not expect the Labour Party to move incrementally, smoothly, and uniformly, to a Marxist-type socialist orientation. We calculate that a really big left-wing advance in the Labour Party will lead to a large right wing splitting off, or the right wing making a huge purge of the left to pre-empt the advance; and we plan to resist. Our guideline is Marx's: we "do not set up any sectarian principles of their own, by which to shape and mould the proletarian movement... [we] are distinguished from the other working-class parties by this only: 1. In the national struggles of the proletarians of the different countries, [we] point out and bring to the front the common interests of the entire proletariat, independently of all nationality. 2. In the various stages of development which the struggle of the working class against the bourgeoisie has to pass through, [we] always and everywhere represent the interests of the movement as a whole... [we] are on the one hand, practically, the most advanced and resolute section of the working-class parties of every country, that section which pushes forward all others". We are an "independent" political organisation in the sense of having our own ideas, worked out independently, distinct from what may be handed down; but the other groupings have the right to that "independence" too, and if they fail to be "independent" it is for lack of their own will and coherence, not because any rule should preclude it. "Independence" here doesn't mean standing aside.

Our route is more laborious than the route of nudging, seeking advancement in the broad movement, and hoping that the leaders will then "deliver". But the extra labour is necessary. As Frederick Engels put it: "The time of surprise attacks, of revolutions carried through by small conscious minorities at the head of masses lacking consciousness is past. Where it is a question of a complete transformation of the social organisation, the masses themselves must also be in on it, must themselves already have grasped what is at stake, what they are fighting for, body and soul". That holds whether the "surprise attack" on capitalism is a military stunt (as Engels had in mind) or an operation of deftly inserting a left-winger at the head of the Labour Party and wriggling them into Downing Street on a prospectus presented as only "anti-austerity" but which we hope cunningly to nudge forward into socialism. People come to grasp "what is at stake" only by discussion and being convinced. That work can sometimes, in the midst of great struggles, be done very fast; but it can never be bypassed. It has to be done all the time and honestly, whether progress is fast or for the moment slow, or otherwise there will be no body capable of organising the discussion with and the convincing of sudden huge numbers mobilised when the great struggles come.

The term "revolutionary" is not much used now to describe the feistier wing of the left. Even the term "radical", adopted since the 1990s as a softer-sounding alternative, now suffers from being widely used as a synonym for "violent Islamist". But surely, at least, we need some better terms to distinguish the feisty left from low-ambition small-steps types than the downright meaningless "transformative" or "transformational".

The real problem with the term "revolutionary" is that in earlier days of the socialist movement it evoked the French Revolution of 1789-93, or the Russian Revolution of 1917, great democratic, emancipatory movements. Now the models of "revolution" first to young people's minds may be the Iranian clericalist revolution of 1979 or the Khmer Rouge overturn of 1975 in Cambodia. The word "revolution" has suffered from abuse, like the words "socialism", or "democracy" for that matter. Even in the *Chartist* article, written by someone knowledgeable, "revolution" is counterposed to "long democratic traditions", as if democratic openings make rapid and comprehensive social change more difficult or remote. In fact, they make it easier, by making it easier for workers to organise, to discuss, and to gain political experience and knowledge.

Yet the term "revolution" still has broad enough connotations for Bernie Sanders, in the USA, to describe his aim as a "revolution", or the Hong Kong movement since 2016 to use the slogan "Liberate Hong Kong, revolution of our times". Yes, our aim is a workers', socialist, revolution. The word "revolution" here has three dimensions. We want not just small modifications, not just to mitigate capitalism piecemeal — but a big move from private ownership of productive wealth and a bureaucratic and militarised state dominated by those private owners to collective ownership and democratic management of productive wealth, with a democratic "semi-state" attuned to workers' control.

The tiger of capitalism cannot be skinned claw by claw. The decisive change must be rapid and comprehensive, and cannot be achieved by an arithmetical sum of small increments spread over a long time. Serious reforms can be won within capitalism, and sustained for long periods; a workers' regime after a revolution would still be, as Marx put it, "in every respect, economically, morally, and intellectually, still stamped with the birthmarks of the old society from whose womb it emerges", and could progress towards full socialism only over years and generations; but the core change can happen only through an abrupt taking of power from one social class (the capitalist plutocrats) by another (the working class). As Marx put it, "revolution is necessary, not only because the ruling class cannot be overthrown in any other way, but also because the class overthrowing it can only in a revolution succeed in ridding itself of all the muck of ages and become fitted to found society anew".

The third dimension is that of educating ourselves to be prepared for counter-revolutionary capitalist violence. As James P Cannon put it: "It is the opinion of all Marxists that [social revolution] will be accompanied by violence... The outlived classes'... attempt to defend themselves against the new order, or to suppress by violence the movement for the new order, has resulted in every important social transformation up to now being accompanied by violence. The position of the Marxists is that the most economical and preferable, the most desirable method of social transformation, by all means, is to have it done peacefully... [It is not] absolutely excluded... The lessons of history don't show any important examples in favor of the idea so that you can count upon it. [We have] a prediction that the outlived class, which is put in a minority by the revolutionary growth in the country, will try by violent means to hold on to its privileges against the will of the majority. We... advise the workers to bear this in mind and prepare themselves not to permit the reactionary outlived minority to frustrate the will of the majority".

In fact, even socialists with a more limited idea of socialism, even socialists who calculate that the changes they want can be won by accumulation of increments over a long time, should prepare for counter-revolutionary violence. Revolution is impossible without a sizeable chunk of the armed forces being won over or convinced to stand aside. That winning-over is entirely possible, but is likely to require the pushing-back by force of the counter-revolutionary diehards, who will otherwise keep the hesitant on their side. The counter-revolutionary military coup in Chile in 1973 happened not because the reforming regime there was too bold, but because it was not bold enough, eschewing rank-and-file organising in the armed forces and instead bringing generals into its government in the hope of appeasing them. The 2021 military coup in Myanmar was driven not by the part-civilian government attempting any revolution, but by the military calculating that worker and democratic organisation had been left weak enough for a coup to win.

The October Revolution of 1917 was probably the most bloodless of great revolutions in history, because when the time came for the government of the elected workers' councils to sweep away the unelected Provisional Government, the revolutionaries had already dispersed the old police force and won over the ranks of the old army. It was followed by a civil war, with 14 states sending troops to help the counter-revolutionaries; but the way that could have been averted was by workers' revolution spreading to other countries, not by the Russian revolutionaries seeking only incremental change.

Revolution in a country like Britain in the 21st century will be different from the Russian Revolution of 1917. In Russia, the workers' councils were the first-ever broad elected democratic bodies, as well as being more flexible and responsive and attuned to workers' control than any parliament. Workers' councils have emerged in a wide variety of countries, across the decades since 1917, and in a wide variety of ways. They are likely to emerge in Britain from councils of action formed in strikes and struggles against the existing unelected state machine ousting or paralysing a reforming parliamentary "workers' government", and to gain supremacy because the struggle has shifted the axis of politics away from the old procedures.

Manifestos, policies, and "real change"

The article in the *Chartist* criticises us for "obsession with the October Revolution". We would happily discuss a wider or more flexible concept of working-class revolution, if the article proposed one. It doesn't. Instead, it counterposes hopes of "many Trotskyist policies and demands achieved through... Labour led by Corbyn and McDonnell".

The 2017 and 2019 manifestos were surely better than anything from Blair, Brown, or Miliband. They promised essentially:

• to repair many of the cuts in services and benefits made by Tory governments after 2010 (though, in the 2017 manifesto, not the cuts in local government services)

• to remove university tuition fees (introduced by Blair in 1999 at £1,000 a year, increased in 2006-7 to £3,000, and then by the Tories and Lib Dems in 2010 to £9,000, for England)

• to restore some public ownership of utilities.

The 2019 manifesto also promised much better climate policies. That aside, essentially the manifestos promised to wind back many of the Tory social counter-reforms since 2010, a few of Blair's, one or two of Thatcher's, and so to restore British social conditions to something nearer 1979, while keeping gains since then like same-sex marriage rights and generally improved technology and real wages. That's assuming that a Corbyn government would have carried out all the manifesto policies in full, despite capitalist resistance, and despite the Parliamentary Labour Party still being dominated by right-wingers. The assumption was always unlikely unless there was a vigorous push to the left from the base of the labour movement.

Both manifestos promised to repeal the Tories' Trade Union Act 2016. Despite repeated Labour Party conference votes to repeal all anti-union laws, neither manifesto promised to restore union and workers' rights to their level before Thatcher, though the 2019 manifesto promised vaguely to "remove unnecessary restrictions on industrial action" and specifically to "allow trade unions to use secure electronic and workplace ballots" (rather than the unwieldy postal ballots insisted on by Thatcher legislation). Again despite a Labour Party conference vote, in 2019, even the 2019 manifesto would not promise to restore the free movement of people between Britain and the EU27 threatened and now destroyed by Brexit.

No-one could have got much more left-wing manifestos through the actual Labour Party of 2017, or 2019? Maybe. It was well worth fighting for the manifestos' reforms, or pushings-back of counter-reforms. Back in the late 19th century, British Marxists made their main campaign one for a legal eight-hour limit on the working day. We want reforms, and we want to use parliamentary channels to their maximum to win those reforms.

But the restoration of social frameworks to early-1980s levels is not socialism. It is not "many Trotskyist policies". It is not an easier way to achieve something comparable to what the October Revolution of 1917 achieved in a different way.

To win the restorations would have emboldened workers, and plausibly led to further demands welling up from the ranks to go beyond Corbyn's limits. But only to the extent that within those ranks, in the workplaces, in the neighbourhoods, there had been socialists with regular week-by-week activity arguing for, explaining, and popularising those further demands, preparing the ground even at a time when most workers thought even the manifesto promises a long shot. That's what Workers' Liberty did and continues to do.

Globalisation

An incrementalist policy was more plausible in the 1970s. Social reforms won over the years, such as those legislated by Labour in Britain in 1945-50, had largely "stuck". Conservatives had resigned themselves to continuing those reforms, indeed sometimes expanding them. It is less plausible today. Despite what the *Chartist* article implies, little-by-little, rely-on-parliamentary-leaders, socialism has less favourable conditions today, not more favourable. Individual governments are under great pressure from the more fluid movements of globally-mobile capital and faster-moving and more enveloping world markets.

Much of the talk by reformists of constraints from globalisation is exaggerated. Reforms can still be won. But the counter-pressures have increased, not reduced. And the shift from standard 1990s neoliberalism since 2008 has more often been towards right-wing nationalist and authoritarian courses (Trump, Erdogan, Modi, Orban...) The scope for large changes to be won by pushing existing favourable trends a bit further, rather than by the more laborious route of overturn via a workers' mobilisation from below, is narrowing, not expanding.

In 2015 Syriza won office in Greece on a prospectus more radical than Corbyn-era Labour's. It faced obstruction from EU institutions; but then Corbyn-era Labour in office would probably have faced equally or more obstruction from the world financial markets, and there was visible potential for workers' solidarity across the EU countries to push the EU institutions to back off. Syriza did not mobilise that solidarity. Within a few months it was negotiating another austerity plan for Greece. It made some marginal reforms, but only marginal. Jacinda Ardern's Labour government in New Zealand has won credit for its handling of the Covid pandemic, but on social issues it has done not much more than the solidly bourgeois government in Taiwan which has handled the pandemic well too. As Ben Peterson reported on the *Jacobin* website (October 2020):

"The government announced a workplace relations reform called Fair Pay Agreements (FPAs). FPAs were supposed to allow workers and unions to negotiate minimum standards across whole industries, alongside existing enterprise bargaining... However, the introduction of FPAs was first delayed and subsequently referred back... In recent years, poverty rates have skyrocketed... Yet [a] working group's report was mothballed and almost all of its recommendations ignored... Ardern also set up KiwiBuild, a state-backed programme to build affordable housing for first-home buyers... By August 2020, only 452 homes were built..."

In Britain, in November 1981 even something so modest as a new low-fares public transport regime for London, pushed by the then left-wing Ken Livingstone as leader of the Greater London Council, was stopped by being ruled illegal by the courts. In 1974, when the Labour government was far from radical, still (so it was later revealed) "fairly senior [army] officers [made] suggestions that perhaps, if things got terribly bad, the army would have to do something about it." With the House of Lords, the courts, the monarchy, and the unelected civil service chiefs, the British state has great resources to deflect a reforming government long before it comes to using the army.

Reducing the socialist perspective to one of hopes of "many Trotskyist policies" being carried out by Corbyn if he should win office, dismissing alternatives as "obsession with the October Revolution", thus means chopping it down to something which offers no more to the rank-and-file worker than unstable mitigations and requires from them no more than modest support. As Rosa Luxemburg put it long ago: "People who pronounce themselves in favour of the method of legislative reform in place and in contradistinction to the conquest of political power and social revolution, do not really choose a more tranquil, calmer and slower road to the same goal, but a different goal. Instead of taking a stand for the establishment of a new society they take a stand for surface modifications of the old society".

Different limitations combined to stunt the Corbyn surge: scaling-down of socialist perspectives; reluctance for substantive debate; the lack of urgency about getting beyond social-media snippets to long-form debate, finding a way to knit together sporadic street protest and regular week-by-week activities, drawing in young people. That is what went wrong with Corbynism. That is what has to be put right if we are to develop the potential which still exists in Labour's new ranks and surely exists longer-term in the broader working class. To put it right it is more laborious than reliance on waiting and hoping for a left-wing prime minister, but more productive.

We work to impose on the ruling class the sentiment that, as the Tory MP Quintin Hogg said in February 1943, "if you do not give the people social reform, they are going to give you social revolution"; and then, when we win those reforms, to press on for more. That tack does not promise instant, quick, easy success. It promises something like Randolph Churchill's description (*Fortnightly Review*, May 1883) of Disraeli's career: "Failure, failure, failure, partial success, renewed failure, ultimate and complete triumph..." Better than the conformist-Corbynite scenario: partial success, illusory success, illusory success, confusion and retreat, rout and abdication...

Study, Propagandise, Organise!

MORE FROM WORKERS' LIBERTY
Order from workersliberty.org/publications

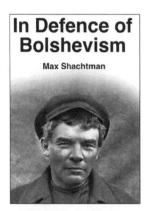

In Defence of Bolshevism

Max Shachtman

Defending the Bolsheviks and their relevance today. 312 pages, **£10**

THE RUSSIAN REVOLUTION: WHEN WORKERS TOOK POWER

PAUL VERNADSKY

The 1917 revolution's real history, and lessons. 374 pages, **£12**

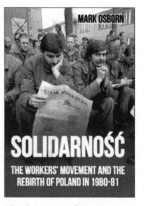

MARK OSBORN

SOLIDARNOŚĆ

THE WORKERS' MOVEMENT AND THE REBIRTH OF POLAND IN 1980-81

The history of Solidarność, from its dawn until the coup. 116 pages, **£5**

THAT'S FUNNY, YOU DON'T LOOK ANTI-SEMITIC

STEVE COHEN

A socialist dissection of Left antisemitism. Third edition, 212 pages, **£5**

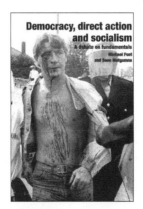

Democracy, direct action and socialism
A debate on fundamentals
Michael Foot and Sean Matgamna

A debate on reform, revolution, Labour, democracy, more. 107 pages, **£5**

The left in disarray

Sean Matgamna

WE ARE ALL HIZBULLAH
BOYCOTT ISRAEL

Critical history of the disoriented left, and the way forward. 408 pages, **£12**

The Miners'
Strike 1984-5
£9

Fate of the Russian Revolution
Vol 1: **£8**   Vol 2: **£20**

1919: Strikes,
struggles, soviets
£4

For a society based
on solidarity, social
ownership of industry,
and democracy.
182 pages, **£5**

A socialist approach
within recent "waves" of
feminism.
102 pages, **£5**

Otto Rühle's abridged
version of Capital is a
good lead-in for the full
book.
131 pages, **£6**

In an Era of Wars
and Revolutions
£9

Class Politics
and Anarchism
£5

Gramsci in
Context
£6

Can Socialism
Make Sense?
£8